First World War
and Army of Occupation
War Diary
France, Belgium and Germany

29 DIVISION
Divisional Troops
Royal Army Veterinary Corps
18 Mobile Veterinary Section
1 February 1916 - 30 October 1919

WO95/2297/3

The Naval & Military Press Ltd
www.nmarchive.com
Published in association with The National Archives

Published by

The Naval & Military Press Ltd

Unit 10 Ridgewood Industrial Park,
Uckfield, East Sussex,
TN22 5QE England
Tel: +44 (0) 1825 749494

www.naval-military-press.com
www.nmarchive.com

This diary has been reprinted in facsimile from the original. Any imperfections are inevitably reproduced and the quality may fall short of modern type and cartographic standards.

Contents

Document type	Place/Title	Date From	Date To
Heading	WO95/2297-3		
Heading	29th Division Divl Troops 18th Mobile Vety Section Feb 1916 To Oct 1919		
War Diary	Mudros	01/02/1916	29/02/1916
War Diary	Suez	01/03/1916	19/03/1916
War Diary	France	20/03/1916	21/03/1916
War Diary	Pontremy	22/03/1916	31/03/1916
War Diary	L'Etoile	01/04/1916	01/04/1916
War Diary	Beauquesne	02/04/1916	03/04/1916
War Diary	Acheux	04/04/1916	30/04/1916
War Diary	Acheux	01/05/1916	23/05/1916
War Diary	Louvencourt	24/05/1916	30/06/1916
Heading	War Diary of 18th Mobile Veterinary Section From July 1st 1916 to July 31st 1916 (Volume)		
War Diary	Louvencourt	01/07/1916	31/07/1916
Heading	War Diary of 18th Mobile Veterinary Section From August 1st 1916 to August 31st 1916 (Volume)		
War Diary	Poperinghe	01/08/1916	31/08/1916
Heading	War Diary of 18th Mobile Veterinary Section from 1-9-16 to 30-9-16 Volume 7		
War Diary	Poperinghe	01/09/1916	30/09/1916
Heading	War Diary of Capt C.M. Stewart O.C. 18th Mob. Vety. Section. From 1st Oct. 1916 to 31st Oct 1916 Vol 8		
Heading	War Diary		
War Diary	Poperinghe	01/10/1916	07/10/1916
War Diary	Corbie	08/10/1916	09/10/1916
War Diary	Ribemont	10/10/1916	18/10/1916
War Diary	Albert	19/10/1916	31/10/1916
Heading	War Diary of Capt. C.M. Stewart O.C. 18th Mobile Section From 1st Nov 1916 to 30 Nov 1916 Volume No 23		
War Diary	Albert Corbie	01/11/1916	16/11/1916
War Diary	Albert Carnoy	17/11/1916	30/11/1916
War Diary	War Diary of Capt. C.M. Stewart OC 18th M.V.S. From 1-12-16 To 31-12-16 Vol 10		
War Diary	Carnoy	01/12/1916	31/12/1916
Heading	War Diary of Captain C M Stewart OC 18th M.V.S. From 1-1-17 To 31-1-17 Vol Number X		
War Diary	Oissy	01/01/1917	12/01/1917
War Diary	Corbie	13/01/1917	16/01/1917
War Diary	Carnoy	17/01/1917	31/01/1917
Heading	War Diary of Capt. CM Stewart OC 18th M.V.S. Month of February 1917 Vol No X		
War Diary	Carnoy	01/02/1917	28/02/1917
Heading	War Diary of Capt C.M. Stewart OC 18th M. V. S. For Month of March 1917 Vol Number X		
War Diary	Carnoy	01/03/1917	04/03/1917
War Diary	Heilly	05/03/1917	20/03/1917
War Diary	Oissy	21/03/1917	30/03/1917
War Diary	Vignacourt	31/03/1917	31/03/1917

Heading	War Diary of Capt C.M. Stewart OC 18th M.V.S. For Month Of April 1917 Volumn No X		
War Diary	Vignacourt	01/04/1917	01/04/1917
War Diary	Beauval	02/04/1917	02/04/1917
War Diary	Lucheux	03/04/1917	05/04/1917
War Diary	Bavincourt	06/04/1917	12/04/1917
War Diary	Agnez	13/04/1917	30/04/1917
Heading	War Diary of Captain C.M. Stewart OC 18th M.V.S. From 1.5.17 To 31.5.17 Vol No X		
War Diary	Couin	01/05/1917	31/05/1917
Heading	War Diary of Capt C.M. Stewart OC 18th M.V.S. From 1-6-17 To 30-6-17 Vol Number X		
War Diary	Achicourt	01/06/1917	30/06/1917
Heading	War Diary of No. 18 Mobile Vety Section Volume No 3		
War Diary	Vox Vrie Farm	01/07/1917	21/07/1917
War Diary	Proven	22/07/1917	31/07/1917
Heading	War Diary of Capt. CM Stewart OC 18 M.V.S. From 1-8-17 To 31-8-17 Volume No X		
War Diary	Proven	01/08/1917	08/08/1917
War Diary	St Sixte	09/08/1917	31/08/1917
Heading	War Diary of Captain CM Stewart OC 18th M.V.S From 1-9-17 To 30-9-17 Volume No X		
War Diary	Proven	01/09/1917	30/09/1917
Heading	War Diary of Captain G Gordon OC 18th M V S From 1-10-17 To 31-10-17 Vol No X		
War Diary	I Camp	01/10/1917	06/10/1917
War Diary	Elverdinghe	07/10/1917	11/10/1917
War Diary	Gards Camps	12/10/1917	17/10/1917
War Diary	Basseux	18/10/1917	31/10/1917
Heading	War Diary of Captain G Gordon OC 18th M.V.S From 1-11-17 To 30-11-17 Vol No X		
War Diary	Basseux	01/11/1917	16/11/1917
War Diary	Bapaume	17/11/1917	18/11/1917
War Diary	Moislain Nurlu	19/11/1917	20/11/1917
War Diary	Dessart Wood	21/11/1917	30/11/1917
Heading	War Diary of Captain G Gordon OC 18th M.V.S From 1-12-17 To 31-12-17 Vol No X		
War Diary	Nurlu	01/12/1917	05/12/1917
War Diary	Bapaume	06/12/1917	06/12/1917
War Diary	Contirelle Le Convey	07/12/1917	17/12/1917
War Diary	Couroy Sur Canche	18/12/1917	19/12/1917
War Diary	Fressin	20/12/1917	20/12/1917
War Diary	Preures	21/12/1917	31/12/1917
Heading	War Diary of Captain G Gordon OC 18th M V S 29 Division From 1-1-18 To 31-1-18 Volume No X		
War Diary	Preures	01/01/1918	03/01/1918
War Diary	Fruquembergues	04/01/1918	04/01/1918
War Diary	Wizernes	05/01/1918	15/01/1918
War Diary	Zimerzeel	16/01/1918	17/01/1918
War Diary	Vlamertinghe	18/01/1918	31/01/1918
Heading	War Diary of Capt G Gordon OC 18th MVS From 1-2-18 To 28-2-18 Volume No X		
War Diary	Vlamertinghe	01/02/1918	28/02/1918
Heading	War Diary of Captain G Gordon OC 18th M.V.S. From 1-3-18 To 31-3-18 Volume No X		

War Diary	Watou	01/03/1918	07/03/1918
War Diary	(S28) GS.b. 7.6.	08/03/1918	31/03/1918
Heading	War Diary of Capt G Gordon OC 18th M V S From 1-4-18 To 30-4-18 Volume No X		
War Diary	G 5B76	01/04/1918	02/04/1918
War Diary	Brandhoek	03/04/1918	09/04/1918
War Diary	Pont Le Parc	10/04/1918	11/04/1918
War Diary	Castre	12/04/1918	12/04/1918
War Diary	St. Sylvestre Cappel	13/04/1918	17/04/1918
War Diary	Hondeghem	18/04/1918	27/04/1918
War Diary	Staple	28/04/1918	29/04/1918
War Diary	Sercus	30/04/1918	30/04/1918
Heading	War Diary of Capt G. Gordon OC 18th M.V.S From 1-5-18 to 31-5-18 Volume No X		
War Diary	Sercus	01/05/1918	31/05/1918
Heading	War Diary of Captain G Gordon OC 18th M.V.S From 1-6-18 to 30-6-18 Volume No X		
War Diary	Sercus	01/06/1918	21/06/1918
War Diary	Bandringham	22/06/1918	22/06/1918
War Diary	Wardrecques	23/06/1918	21/07/1918
War Diary	Oxelaere	22/07/1918	31/07/1918
Heading	War Diary of Captain G. Gordon OC 18th M.V.S From 1-8-18 to 31-8-18 Vol No X		
War Diary	Bavinchove	01/08/1918	03/08/1918
War Diary	U24-C.9.6	04/08/1918	31/08/1918
Heading	War Diary of Capt G Gordon OC 18th M.V.S. From 1-9-18 To 30-9-18 Vol No X		
War Diary	U24. A56	01/09/1918	02/09/1918
War Diary	Nr Wallon-Cappel	03/09/1918	07/09/1918
War Diary	27/W 24. b. 24	08/09/1918	10/09/1918
War Diary	Haze Brouck	11/09/1918	17/09/1918
War Diary	27/F.22. b. 55	18/09/1918	26/09/1918
War Diary	Brown Farm.	27/09/1918	27/09/1918
War Diary	28/H. 11 a.0.9.	28/09/1918	30/09/1918
War Diary	War Diary of Capt G Gordon OC 18th M.V.S. From 1-10-18 to 31-10-18 Vol No X		
War Diary	Oppus Reamerlinghe Rd.	01/10/1918	11/10/1918
War Diary	Oppus Menin	12/10/1918	15/10/1918
War Diary	Beceleare	16/10/1918	16/10/1918
War Diary	Dadizeele	17/10/1918	17/10/1918
War Diary	Legeghem	18/10/1918	20/10/1918
War Diary	Steenbeek	21/10/1918	22/11/1918
War Diary	29/H 14 C 24	23/10/1918	27/10/1918
War Diary	Mouvaux	28/10/1918	31/10/1918
Heading	War Diary of Capt G. Gordon OC 18th M.V.S. From 1st 11-18 to 30-11-18 Vol No X		
War Diary	Mouvaux	01/11/1918	07/11/1918
War Diary	Rolleghem	08/11/1918	10/11/1918
War Diary	St Genoa	11/11/1918	14/11/1918
War Diary	Horbecq	15/11/1918	18/11/1918
War Diary	Enghien	19/11/1918	20/11/1918
War Diary	Tubecq	21/11/1918	22/11/1918
War Diary	Braine-L-Alleud	23/11/1918	24/11/1918
War Diary	Ottignes	25/11/1918	26/11/1918
War Diary	Nil-Abbesse	27/11/1918	27/11/1918
War Diary	Grand	28/11/1918	28/11/1918

War Diary	Roser Huy	29/11/1918	30/11/1918
Heading	War Diary of Capt Gordon R.A.V.C. OC 18th M.V.S. From 1-12-18 to 31-12-18 Vol No X		
War Diary	Anthisnes	01/12/1918	02/12/1918
War Diary	Niverre	03/12/1918	03/12/1918
War Diary	Malmian	04/12/1918	04/12/1918
War Diary	Katter Herberg	05/12/1918	06/12/1918
War Diary	Strufenborn	07/12/1918	07/12/1918
War Diary	Zulpich	08/12/1918	08/12/1918
War Diary	Epperin	09/12/1918	13/12/1918
War Diary	Bensberg	14/12/1918	21/12/1918
War Diary	Berg Gladbach	22/12/1918	31/12/1918
Heading	War Diary of Capt G Gordon OC 18th MVS From 1-1-19 to 31-1-19 vol No X		
War Diary	Berg Gladbach	01/01/1919	25/03/1919
Heading	War Diary of Capt G Gordon OC 18th MVS From 1-3-19 to 31-3-19 Vol No X		
War Diary	Berg Gladbach	01/03/1919	31/03/1919
War Diary	Berg Gladbach	01/04/1919	30/04/1919
Heading	War Diary of Capt Hill OC 18th MVS from 1-5-19 to 31-5-19 Vol No X		
War Diary	Berg Gladbach	01/05/1919	31/05/1919
Heading	War Diary of Capt Hill OC 18 MVS From 1-6-19 To 30-6-19 Vol No X IIV		
War Diary	Berg Gladbach	01/06/1919	30/06/1919
War Diary	War Diary of Capt Hill OC 18th MVS From 1-7-19 To 31-7-19 Volume No XII		
War Diary	Berg Gladbach	01/07/1919	31/07/1919
Heading	War Diary of Capt Edgar OC 18th MVS From 1-8-19 To 31-8-19 Vol No X VIII		
War Diary	Berg Gladbach	01/08/1919	31/08/1919
Heading	War Diary of Major Belt OC 18th MVS From 1-9-19 To 30.9.19 Volume No X 9		
War Diary	Berg Gladbach	01/09/1919	30/09/1919
War Diary	Berg Gladbach	01/10/1919	31/10/1919
War Diary	Berg Gladbach	21/10/1919	30/10/1919

29TH DIVISION
DIVL TROOPS

18TH MOBILE VETY SECTION

~~MAR 1916-DEC 1919~~

FEB 1916 TO OCT 1919

Instructions regarding War Diaries and Intelligence Summaries are contained in F. S. Regs., Part II. and the Staff Manual respectively. Title pages will be prepared in manuscript.

WAR DIARY
or
INTELLIGENCE SUMMARY.
(Erase heading not required.)

Army Form C. 2118.

18th Mob. Vety Sect.
Certified true copy of War Diary for month of FEB.
[signature] Captain

Place	Date	Hour	Summary of Events and Information	Remarks and references to Appendices
MUDROS.	Feb 1st	1916	—	
	2nd		1st Corpl. BALLENTYNE & Dr SIMPSON attached from A.S.C.	
	3rd		—	
	4th		—	
	5th		—	
	6th		—	
	7th		—	
	8th		ORDERS received to EMBARK on the 10th	
	9th		EMBARKED on S.S. BOHEMIAN. 46 Horses 25 MULES. 1 Officer 40 MEN including attached.	
	10th		—	
	11th			
	12th		Sailed.	
	13th		arrived Alexandria	
	14th		DISEMBARKED & received orders to Proceed to Suez. Handed Sick into 11th Vety Hospital 39 Horses 25 mules. Corpls. North & WILLIAMS PTES. COOK. CLARKE & Dr HEELER A.S.C. rejoined Section. Corpl VAUGHAN rejoined 16th Vety Hospital Sergt COLLINGS & PTE SPENSER transferred to 11th Vety Hospital	
	15th			
	16th			
	17th		Entrained at SABARRH Station for SUEZ	
	18th		ARRIVED Suez & proceeded to Camp	
	19th		—	
	20th		A.D.V.S. 29th DIV visited Section	
	21st		—	
	22nd		—	
	23rd		VISIT of D.D.V.S M.E.F.	
	24th		No 508 Corpl. S.H. North transferred to 87th Inf Bde for duty	
	25th		No 5541 acting Sergt T.W. Cook & No 5668 R. ORMISTON. Transferred to 147 Bde RFA for duty	
	26th			
	27th			
	28th			
	29th			

[signature] Capt AVC
OC 18th Mob Vety Sect

1577 Wt. W10791/1773 500,000 1/15 D. D. & L. A.D.S.S./Forms/C. 2118.

Army Form C. 2118.

Instructions regarding War Diaries and Intelligence Summaries are contained in F. S. Regs., Part II. and the Staff Manual respectively. Title pages will be prepared in manuscript.

WAR DIARY
or
INTELLIGENCE SUMMARY.
(Erase heading not required.)

18th Mobile Veterinary Section

Place	Date	Hour	Summary of Events and Information	Remarks and references to Appendices
SUEZ	MARCH 1st		—	
	2nd		CAPT. C M STEWART rejoined the section on returning from leave	
	3rd			
	4th		—	
	5th			
	6th		SERGT W. T. BISS. + 4 MEN went as conducting party to 20th Vety Hospital abassia. with 22 MULES 18 Horses	
	7th		ORDERS received to ~~[illegible]~~ entrain Section riding horses (3).	
	8th			
	9th	2 AM.	Corpl. S. WILLIAMS + 2 MEN. entrained with 3 Horses for ALEXANDRIA. SERGT. W T. BISS + 4 MEN rejoined section. SEVEN (7) men arrived from 20th Vety Hospital as reinforcements. 4 Horses L.D. transferred to 29th DIV. TRAIN.	
	10th.		(2) two limbered G. S. wagons transferred to 29th DIV. TRAIN.	
	11th		1 officer. 23 other Ranks embarked on H. M. T. WARILDA. SAILED 5 PM	
	12th	~~[illegible]~~	arrived Port SAID 9 AM.	
	13th		PORT SAID	
	14th		SAILED 7 PM.	
	15th			
	16th		~~Lecture~~ Lecture on ASPHYXIATING GAS.	
	17th		—	
	18th		—	
	19th		arrived MARSEILLES 6 PM.	
FRANCE	20th		Disembarked 6 30 AM. Entrained 10 30 AM.	
	21st		on the Train	
PONTREMY	22nd		arrived at PONT. REMY & Proceeded to BILLETS. CAPT. C. M. STEWART took over from CAPT ARMSTRONG as Disembarcation Vety officer.	
	23rd		Drew 4 DRAUGHT Horses & 2 LIMBERED G. S. WAGONS from ADV. Horse Transport Depot	
	24th		—	
	25th			
	26th		CAPT C M STEWART proceeded on leave. ANTOINE. LLORCA joined the section as interpreter.	

1577 Wt. W10791/1773 500,000 1/15 D. D. & L. A.D.S.S./Forms/C. 2118.

C M Stewart, Capt AVC
OC 18th M. V. S.

Instructions regarding War Diaries and Intelligence Summaries are contained in F. S. Regs., Part II. and the Staff Manual respectively. Title pages will be prepared in manuscript.

WAR DIARY
or
INTELLIGENCE SUMMARY.
(*Erase heading not required.*)

Army Form C. 2118.

18th Mobile Veterinary Section

Place	Date	Hour	Summary of Events and Information	Remarks and references to Appendices
PONT. REMY	MARCH 27th	—	28 HORSES. 13 MULES evacuated to NO 22 VETY HOSPITAL ABBEVILLE → 1 Limbered S.S. WAGON handed to Advanced Horse Transport DEPÔT. Received One Horse AMBULANCE from NO 5 Vety Hospital	
	28th		—	
	29th		—	
	30th		—	
	31st		1 Horse 31st Division collected from WANEL by + transferred by AMBULANCE to 22nd VETY Hospital ABBEVILLE. Section Moved to L'Etoile (L'ETOILE)	

A.M. Stewart Capt. A.V.C.
OC 18th Mob Vety Sect.

APRIL

Instructions regarding War Diaries and Intelligence Summaries are contained in F. S. Regs., Part II. and the Staff Manual respectively. Title pages will be prepared in manuscript.

WAR DIARY
or
INTELLIGENCE SUMMARY.
(Erase heading not required.)

18th MOBILE VETERINARY SECTION.
No.
Date 13-6-16

Army Form C. 2118.

Place	Date	Hour	Summary of Events and Information	Remarks and references to Appendices
L'ETOILE	1st		Marched to BEAUQUESNE. CAPT. C.M STEWART rejoined section	
BEAUQUESNE	2nd		—	
	3rd		marched to ACHEUX + took over billets of 48th M.V.S.	
ACHEUX	4th		—	
	5th		—	
	6th		—	
	7th		—	
	8th		13 Horses 1 MULE to 22nd Vety Hospital	
	9th		—	
	10th		—	
	11th		—	
	12th			
	13th		Pte HUGHES admitted to 89th Fd Amb.	
	14th		13 horses 2 MULES to 22nd Vety Hosp. 4 Men joined from 7th Vety Hospital	
	15th		3 men transferred to 7th Vety Hospital 17 remounts arrived	
	16th		Pte CADLE admitted to 89th Fd Amb.	
	17th		—	
	18th		Board of officers to examine Ptes 2855 MILLAR + 5592 MUIR for appointment to S.S.	
	19th		10 horses + 10 Mules to 22nd Vety Hospital	
	20th		—	
	21st		—	
	22nd		5 Mules + 3 horses to 22nd Vety Hospital	
	23rd			
	24th		—	
	25th		8 horses to 22nd Vety Hospital	
	26th		1 horse 7 mules to 22nd Vety Hospital	
	27th		4 " 4 " " — —	
	28th		—	
	29th		2 mules 6 horses " " "	
	30th		3 horses 5 mules " " "	

C.M. Stewart Captain
OC 18th M.V.S.

1577 Wt. W10791/1773 500,000 1/15 D. D. & L. A.D.S.S./Forms/C. 2118.

MAY.

Instructions regarding War Diaries and Intelligence Summaries are contained in F. S. Regs., Part II. and the Staff Manual respectively. Title pages will be prepared in manuscript.

WAR DIARY
or
INTELLIGENCE SUMMARY.
(*Erase heading not required.*)

18th MOBILE VETERINARY SECTION.
No.
Date 13-6-16

Army Form C. 2118.

29

Vol 2 + 3

Place	Date	Hour	Summary of Events and Information	Remarks and references to Appendices
~~MAY~~	1st		—	
ACHEUX	2nd		Pte A BUNYAN (No 1307) addt to Hospital No 1737 Pte HILLIER joined section from 7th Vety Hospital	
	3rd		6 horses 1 Mule to 22nd Vety Hospital	
	4th			
	5th		18 " 6 " " — — —	
	6th		No 13077 rejoined section from Hospital	
	7th		D.V.S. 4th Army visited the section	
	8th		6 horses 3 Mules to 22nd Vety Hospital	
	9th			
	10th		8 " — — — —	
	11th		— "	
	12th		—	
	13th		—	
	14th		8 "	
	15th		Capt C M Stewart — proceeded on Leave —	
	16th		—	
	17th		—	
	18th		SS MILLAR (2885) to No1 Vety Hospital	
	19th		—	
	20th		—	
	21st		—	
	22nd		6 horses to 22nd Vety Hospital	
LOUVENCOURT.	23rd		Section moved to Louvencourt & took over billets of 31st M.V.S.	
	24th		—	
	25th		Capt C M. Stewart rejoined section from leave	
	26th		—	
	27th		8 Horses to 22nd Vety Hospital	
	28th		—	
	29th		7 " 1 MULE to Vety "	
	30th		—	
	31st		Dr HEELER (T4.04407) addt to 87th Fd Ambulance	C M Stewart Captain

1577 Wt. W10791/1773 500,000 1/15 D. D. & L. A.D.S.S./Forms/C. 2118.

June

Instructions regarding War Diaries and Intelligence Summaries are contained in F. S. Regs., Part II. and the Staff Manual respectively. Title pages will be prepared in manuscript.

WAR DIARY
or
INTELLIGENCE SUMMARY.
(Erase heading not required.)

18th MOBILE VETERINARY SECTION.
No. ....
Date 2-7-16

Army Form C. 2118. 29

Vol 4

Place	Date	Hour	Summary of Events and Information	Remarks and references to Appendices
LOUVENCOURT.	1st	—	10 horses to 22nd Vety Hosp. No 508 Corpl North attached from 17th Inf. Bde	
	2nd		—	
	3rd		No 7?52 Pte LAKE, A. joined Section	
	4th		7 horses 3 Mules 2 foals to 22nd Vety Hosp.	
	5th		—	
	6th		T4.044077 Dr. S. HEELER rejoined from Hospital	
	7th		—	
	8th		6 Horses 1 mule to 22nd Vety Hosp.	
	9th		Pte POPPLE rejoined from leave	
	10th		—	
	11th		No 508 Corpl. S.H NORTH proceeded to No 23 Vety Hosp for duty 5 horses	
	12th		3 mules to No 7 Vety Hosp. No 5562 Pte BRYANT. C. proceeded on leave	
	13th		No 5238 Corpl CLARKE. G rejoined from leave	
	14th		6 horses 2 Mules to No 7 Vety Hosp	
	15th			
	16th		5 horses 2 mules to N.7 " "	
	17th			
	18th		8 " to "	
	19th		A.D.V.S. visited Section. 17 horses 1 mule 2 foals to No 7 Vety Hosp	
	20th		1 Sergt 9 Men attached from 22nd Vety Hosp 13 horses 1 mule to No 7 V. H.	
	21st			
	22nd		44 Horses 2 Mules to No 7 V. H	
	23rd		5 horses 3 — to — — — — Corpl. S. Williams + Pte P Perry to B Collecting Station	
	~~23rd~~		Pte J MAHER + Pte M MUNRO to A Station as advanced dressing parties	
	24th		3 Men to 41st M.V.S. as Horse conducting party	
	25th		10 horses 4 Mules to 7th V H.	
	26th		—	
	27th			
	28th		5 Men to 41st M.V.S. as conducting party	
	29th		62 horses 4 Mules to No 7 V. H.	
	30th			

[signature], Captain.

1577 Wt. W10791/1773 500,000 1/15 D. D. & L. A.D.S.S./Forms/C. 2118.

Vol 5

Confidential

War Diary of

18th Mobile Veterinary Section

From July 1st 1916 to July 31st 1916

(Volume ~~XVII~~)

July 1916.

Instructions regarding War Diaries and Intelligence Summaries are contained in F. S. Regs., Part II. and the Staff Manual respectively. Title pages will be prepared in manuscript.

from 1/7/16 to 31/7/16

Vol. XVII

WAR DIARY of 18th Mob. Vety Sect.
or
~~INTELLIGENCE SUMMARY.~~

(Erase heading not required.)

Army Form C. 2118.

[signature] Captain
OC 18th M.V.S.

Place	Date	Hour	Summary of Events and Information	Remarks and references to Appendices
LOUVENCOURT	1st		9 Horses 1 Mule to No 7 Vety Hospital.	
	2nd		—	
	3rd		1 LD Horse destroyed (Section)	
	4th		A.D.V.S. Visited Section	
	5th		16 Horses 3 Mules to No 7 Vety Hosp.	
	6th		15 " 1 " " 7 " " Personell at collecting posts recalled	
	7th		66?? Pte E Holland Remanded for D.C.M. Orders received to move to Acheux (A.D.V.S. 29th?)	
	8th			
	9th		Section moved to Acheux & took over Billet No 92. 2 attached men to 22 Vety Hosp for duty.	
	10th			
	11th		8 horses to No 7 Vety Hosp.	
	12th		—	
	13th		14 Horses 2 mules to No 7 Vety Hosp.	
	14th		6 " to No 7 Vety Hosp. F.G.C.M. on No 669 Pte C Holland promulgated.	
	15th		3 Men returned to 22nd Vety Hosp. [illegible]	
	16th		15 Horses 1 Mule to 7th Vety Hosp. S.M. [illegible] M.V.S. 7 Horses 1 Mule to 7 Vety Hosp.	
	17th			
	18th		D.D.V.S. Reserve army Visited section	
	19th		15 horses 2 mules to 7 Vety Hosp.	
	20th		—	
	21st		8 " to No 7 Vety Hosp.	
	22nd		—	
	23rd		10 " 6 mules to No 7 Vety Hosp	
	24th		26 " 2 " " 7 " "	
	25th		Sergt Evans (No 2630) left section to arrange billets in advance.	
	26th		1 Sergt & 9 Men arrived from No 1 Vety Hosp. & [illegible] to A.D.V.S. 49th Div.	
	27th		Section Marched out at 9 AM. to [illegible] from Beauval at 11 PM to [illegible]	
	28th	4.6	Left [illegible] arrived [illegible] 12 midday marched to Billet at F 30 A sheet 27	
	29th		took over 26 Horses 2 mules from 6th M.V.S. No 2630 Sergt W.J. Evans with 5 men conducting party for	
	30th		45 animals left M.V.S.	
	31st		20 horses & 2 mules by Road to 23rd Vety Hosp. No 2636 L/Cpl C. Williams + 7 Men [illegible]	

Vol 6

Confidential

War Diary
of
18th Mobile Veterinary Section

from August 1st 1916 to August 31st 1916

(Volume ~~VIII~~)

month of August

18th MOBILE VETERINARY SECTION.

WAR DIARY
or
INTELLIGENCE SUMMARY.
(*Erase heading not required.*)

Army Form C. 2118.

Instructions regarding War Diaries and Intelligence Summaries are contained in F. S. Regs., Part II. and the Staff Manual respectively. Title pages will be prepared in manuscript.

Place	Date	Hour	Summary of Events and Information	Remarks and references to Appendices
POPERINGHE	1st		—	
	2nd		D.D.V.S. 2nd Army visited section.	
	3rd		A.D.V.S. 29th Div on leave O.C. 18th M.V.S. appointed acting A.D.V.S.	
	4th			
	5th		—	
	6th			
	7th		15 horses 1 mule to 23 Vety Hosp. ST OMER.	
	8th		—	
	9th		5175 PTE E.W. CHAPPLE admitted to 87th Fd amb.	
	10th		—	
	11th		—	
	12th		—	
	13th		A.D.V.S. 29th Div. returned	
	14th		40 Horses 9 Mules to No 23 Vety Hosp in charge of 1 N.C.O. + 10 men	
	15th		—	
	16th		—	
	17th			
	18th		No 244 PTE CAVE. H.J. attached to section.	
	19th		No 1737 PTE HILLIER. T. + No T4 12749 Dr GREY. E to R.O.D. AUDRUICQ for duty as cleaners.	
	20th		27 Horses + 2 MULES to No 13 Vety Hosp. O.C. 18th M.V.S. in charge of train. Dr GREY + PTE HILLIER returned to section - unsuitable.	
	21st		—	
	22nd		—	
	23rd		No 244 PTE CAVE. H.J. to No 2 Vety Hosp HAVRE.	
	24th		D.D.V.S. 2nd ARMY. inspected section.	
	25th		—	
	26th			
	27th		No 2690 Sergt. BECKETT. F. + PTE HAIME arrived at section.	
	28th		Proceeded to ACHEUX + PTE Haime to Forges LES EAUX.	
	29th		21 Horses 8 mules to No 23 Vety Hosp in charge of 1 N.C.O. 6 Men	
	30th			
	31st			

A McStewart
Captain

1577 Wt. W10791/1773 500,000 1/15 D. D. & L. A.D.S.S./Forms/C. 2118.

29

Vol 7

Confidential

War Diary

of

18th Mobile Veterinary Section

from 1 - 9 - 16 to 30 - 9 - 16.

(Volume ~~9~~)

Instructions regarding War Diaries and Intelligence Summaries are contained in F. S. Regs., Part II. and the Staff Manual respectively. Title pages will be prepared in manuscript.

WAR DIARY
or
~~INTELLIGENCE SUMMARY.~~

(Erase heading not required.)

Army Form C. 2118.

Place	Date	Hour	Summary of Events and Information	Remarks and references to Appendices
POPERINGHE	1st		—	
	2nd		No 2630 Sergt W. J. BISS to ENGLAND on special leave	
	3rd		8 Horses 1 MULE to No 23 Vety Hospital	
	4th		1 Riding Horse drawn from 20th Div. R A details to complete establishment	
	5th		—	
	6th		—	
	7th		—	
	8th		—	
	9th		—	
	10th		14 Horses 6 mules to NO 23 Vety Hosp.	
	11th		—	
	12th		—	
	13th		No 2641 Pte. WAGSTAFF. A. addt to 89th Fd Ambulance. Sgt BISS. W. J. returned from leave	
	14th		No 5238 Corpl Clarke. S. to No 12 Vety Hosp. on course of instruction in STEWART. Capt.	
	15th		—	
	16th		No 5175 PTE CHAPPLE. E.W. to 89th Fd Ambulance	
	17th			
	18th		No T2/12749 Dr. GREY. E. on leave to ENGLAND	
	19th		25 Horses 1 MULE to No 13 Vety Hospital also 74 Horses No 4 Sect 29th D.A.C.	
	20th		—	
	21st		—	
	22nd		—	
	23rd		—	
	24th		—	
	25th		25 Horses 3 mules to NO 13 Vety Hospital. 92 Horse 17th F.A. Bde. to 13 Vety Hosp.	
	26th		—	
	27th		—	
	28th		36 Horses 1 MULE to No 23 Vety Hosp. Dr. Grey returned from leave PTE WAGSTAFF rejoined from Hosp.	
	29th			
	30		—	

G. W. Stewart. Captain
OC 18th M. V. S.

Vol 8

Confidential

War Diary

of

Capt. C. M. Stewart
OC. 18th Mob. Vety. Section.

From 1st Oct 1916 to 31st Oct 1916

Volume No. ~~II~~

~~War Diary~~

OCTOBER

Instructions regarding War Diaries and Intelligence Summaries are contained in F. S. Regs., Part II. and the Staff Manual respectively. Title pages will be prepared in manuscript.

WAR DIARY
or
INTELLIGENCE SUMMARY.
(Erase heading not required.)

Army Form C. 2118.

Place	Date	Hour	Summary of Events and Information	Remarks and references to Appendices
POPERINGHE	1st		—	
	2nd		5 Horses to 23 V H.	
	3rd		—	
	4th		NO 2630 Sgt. BISS. W.J. to CORBIE as Billeting N.C.O.	
	5th		—	
	6th		Handed over Billets + 35 Sick horses to 1/1st West RIDING M.V.S	
	7th		Left Billet 2.30 A.M. + proceeded to PROVEN. Left PROVEN 7 A.M. arrived SALEUX 8.10 P.M. + Proceeded to CORBIE.	
CORBIE	8th		Arrived CORBIE 4 AM + relieved 4th M.V.S	
	9th		—	
RIBEMONT	10th		Left CORBIE for RIBEMONT arriving 2.45 P.M. took over Billet of 40th M.V.S.	
	11th		—	
	12th		—	
	13th		6 H. + 1 Mule to No 7 V. H.	
	14th		—	
	15th		—	
	16th		12 H 1 Mule to NO 7 V H.	
	17th		—	
	18th		NO 232 A/SERGT SKINNER. F appointed A/S/Sergt.	
ALBERT	19th		Left RIBEMONT 1 P.M. Arrived ALBERT 3 P.M. + took over BILLETS of 23rd M.V.S	
	20th		1 NCO 5 MEN attached from NO 23 M.V.S.	
	21st		6 Horses 2 Mules to NO 7 V.H. A/Sergt W.J. BISS (2630) to 87th Inf Bde (temporarily)	
	22nd		—	
	23rd		—	
	24th		—	
	25th		99 ?/Sergt S.H. DOYLE arrived from No 1 C. H. D to complete establishment 6 Horses + 2 Mules to NO 7 V.H.	
	26th		14 H 2 Mules to No 7 V H.	
	27th		A/S. SERGT. F SKINNER to NO 10 V. H.	

C. M. Stewart Captain
OC 10th Mobile Vety Sect

OCTOBER

Instructions regarding War Diaries and Intelligence Summaries are contained in F. S. Regs., Part II. and the Staff Manual respectively. Title pages will be prepared in manuscript.

WAR DIARY
or
INTELLIGENCE SUMMARY.
(Erase heading not required.)

Army Form C. 2118.

Place	Date	Hour	Summary of Events and Information	Remarks and references to Appendices
ALBERT	28th		14 Horses 2 Mules to No 7 V H.	
	29th		16 Horses to No 7 V H.	
	30th		13 " 2 mules to No 7 V. H.	
	31st		33 " 2 mules to No 7 V H	
			B McIlwrick Captain	

1577 Wt. W10791/1773 500,000 1/15 D. D. & L. A.D.S.S./Forms/C. 2118.

Vol 9

Confidential

War Diary

of

Capt. C. M. Stewart,
O.C. 18th Mobile Section

From 1st Nov 1916 to 30 Nov 1916

Volume No 23

Army Form C. 2118.

WAR DIARY
or
~~INTELLIGENCE SUMMARY.~~

(Erase heading not required.)

Instructions regarding War Diaries and Intelligence Summaries are contained in F. S. Regs., Part II. and the Staff Manual respectively. Title pages will be prepared in manuscript.

Place	Date	Hour	Summary of Events and Information	Remarks and references to Appendices
ALBERT.	1st.		Section moved from ALBERT to CORBIE.	
CORBIE.	2nd		1 NCO + 5 men 23rd M.V.S. rejoined their unit. 1 NCO. + 5 men of Section to 1st AUST. M.V.S.	
"	3rd		—	
"	4th		26 Horses 4 Mules to No 7 Vety. Hosp.	
"	5th		27 " 2 " " " 7 " "	
"	6th		3 " 5 " " " 7 " "	
"	7th		4 " 4 " " " 7 " "	
"	8th		8 " 5 " " " 7 " "	
"	9th		—	
"	10th		—	
"	11th		12 " to No 7 Vety Hosp.	
"	12th		6 " 1 mule to No 7 V. H.	
"	13th		—	
"	14th		8 " 4 " " " 7 " "	
"	15th		3 " 1 " " " 7 " "	
"	16th		Section marched to ALBERT.	
ALBERT.	17th		Section marched from ALBERT. to CARNOY.	
CARNOY.	18th		18 Horses 14 mules to No 7 Vety HOSP. PTE WAGSTAFF evact to 87th Fd Amb.	
"	19th		34. " 1 " " " 7 " "	
"	20th		34 " 13 " " " 7 " " S.S. FISH G + PTE CARLEY. J W. joined from 14th Vety Hosp	
"	21st		73 " 5 " " " 7 " "	
"	22nd		57 " — — " 7 " " S.S. MUIR. R transferred to No 14 Vety Hosp PTE PEPPER E on leave.	
	23rd		39 " 3 " " 7 " "	
	24th		45 " 8 " " 7 " "	
	25.		45 " 4 " " 7 " "	
	26.		—	
	27th		36 " 3 " " 7 " "	
	28th		—	
	29th		45 " 5 " " 7 " "	
	30th		21 " 2 " " 7 " "	

A M Stewart Captain
OC 18th M.V.S.

Confidential

War Diary

of

Capt. C. M. Stewart OC 18th. M.V.S.

From 1-12-16 To 31-12-16

Volumn No ~~II~~

Vol 10

Instructions regarding War Diaries and Intelligence Summaries are contained in F. S. Regs., Part II. and the Staff Manual respectively. Title pages will be prepared in manuscript.

WAR DIARY
or
~~INTELLIGENCE SUMMARY.~~
(Erase heading not required.)

Army Form C. 2118.

Place	Date	Hour	Summary of Events and Information	Remarks and references to Appendices
CARNOY	1st		29 H 6 M to No 7 Vet Hospital.	
	2nd		—	
	3rd			
	4th		23 H 3 M - -	
	5th		15 H 6 M - - - -	
	6th		21 H "	
	7th		10 H 11 M. - - - -	
	8th		33 H 1 M - - - -	
	9th		23 H 6 M - - - -	
	10th		25 H 8 M - - - - orders received to proceed to Corbie morning of 12th + to Oissy on 13th.	
	11th			
	12th	6AM	Left CARNOY arrived CORBIE 4 PM	
	13th	8AM	Left CORBIE " OISSY 6 PM. No 996 A/Sergt Doyle S. H placed in arrest	
	14th		—	
	15th		Sergt S H DOYLE remanded for Court martial by Major J. J GRIFFITH D.S.O A.D.V.S	
	~~15th~~		P.A/SERGT. PITMAN A.V.C returned to No 3 Vet. Hosp.	
	16th		PTE 2445 HILL ~~des~~patched to No 2 Vet Hosp	
	17th		PTE 5477 MASON J. returned from leave.	
	18th			
	19th		17 H. 5 M. to No 7 Vety Hosp.	
	20th		No 5508 PTE SIMMS. W.G. returned from leave	
	21st		PTE 704 TENNANT J proceeded on leave 19 H. 5 M to No 7 VET. Hosp.	
	22nd			
	23rd		No 897 PTE PERRY. D. proceeded on leave No 5024 PTE ATWELL J. returned from leave	
	24th			
	25th		F.G.C.M. on 996 Sergt DOYLE. S.H.	
	26th		5474 PTE MUNRO. M. proceeded on leave. Promulgation of Proceedings of F.G.C.M on Sgt Doyle sentence to be reduced to the ranks	
	27th		No 996 PTE DOYLE. S.H. to No 7 Vety Hosp. 28 H. 1 M. to No 7 Vety Hosp	
	28th		L/Corpl POPPLE (No 5653) sent to 88th Inf Bde in relief of Sergt AITKEN on leave	
	29th			
	30th			[illegible] Captain OC 18th M.V.S.
	31st			

1577 Wt. W10791/1773 500,000 1/15 D. D. & L. A.D.S.S./Forms/C. 2118.

Vol XI

Confidential

War Diary

of

Captain C. M. Stewart
OC 18th M.V.S

From 1-1-17 To 31-1-17

Vol Number X.

Instructions regarding War Diaries and Intelligence Summaries are contained in F. S. Regs., Part II. and the Staff Manual respectively. Title pages will be prepared in manuscript.

WAR DIARY

~~or~~

~~INTELLIGENCE SUMMARY.~~

(Erase heading not required.)

Army Form C. 2118.

Place	Date	Hour	Summary of Events and Information	Remarks and references to Appendices
OISSY.	1st	-	Collected 8 horses + 2 mules ~~from~~ left behind by 8th Div in rest area	
	2nd		22 Horses 3 mules evacuated to No 7 Vet Hospital.	
	3rd		—	
	4th		704 PTE TENNANT. J. returned from leave. 1 Horse of 8th Div. collected from SUIBERMESNIL	
	5th			
	6th		—	
	7th		CAPT. C.M. STEWART. proceeded on leave 8 Horses + 4 MULES to NO 7 V.H.	
	8th		897 L/Copl PERRY returned from leave. Orders received to move to CORBIE.	
	9th		5474 PTE. MUNRO. M. returned from leave	
	10th			
	11th			
	12th	7-30AM	moved from OISSY to CORBIE. No 1 Billet for men 37 Billet for Horses	
CORBIE.	13th		7 Horses to NO 7. V.H. No 12859 PTE MINTY arrived from NO 2 V.H.	
	14th		8 mules to - - - No 12859 - MINTY returned to NO 2 V.H. 13023 A/Sergt EPPS J attached.	
	15th		PTE EPPS. returned to No 2 V.H. on reduction from A/Sergt.	
	16th		Left CORBIE 7 A.M. arrived CARNOY 3 P.M. 6 Men of 29th M.V.S. attached	
CARNOY	17th			
	18th		15 Horses 4 Mules to NO 7 V.H. No 2636 Copl WILLIAMS. S. promoted to A/Sergt (paid) authority Local Corps Order No 60 dated 13/1/17.	
	19th		G.O.C. 14th Corps inspected section lines.	
	20th			
	21st		5 Horses + 1 Mule destroyed.	
	22nd		CAPT. C.M. STEWART rejoined section on return from leave. 35 Horses 2 Mules to NO 7 V.H.	
			PTE BUNYAN. A. (No 13077) admitted to 14th Corps Rest Station.	
	23rd		—	
	24th		18 Horses + 2 Mules to NO 7 V.H.	
	25th		—	
	26th		—	
	27th		—	
	28th		—	
	29th		—	
	30th		—	
	31st		—	

[illegible] Captain
OC 18th Mobile Vety Sect.

~~1577~~ Wt. W10791/1773 500,000 1/15 D. D. & L. A.D.S.S./Forms/C. 2118.

Confidential

Vol 12

War Diary

of Capt: C M. Stewart

OC 18th M.V.S.

Month of February 1917

Vol No X.

February 1917.

Instructions regarding War Diaries and Intelligence Summaries are contained in F. S. Regs., Part II. and the Staff Manual respectively. Title pages will be prepared in manuscript.

WAR DIARY

or

~~INTELLIGENCE SUMMARY.~~

(Erase heading not required.)

Army Form C. 2118.

Place	Date	Hour	Summary of Events and Information	Remarks and references to Appendices
CARNOY	1st Feb		—	
	2nd		—	
	3rd		—	
	4th		Orders received to proceed to Heilly 9.2.17 No13077 PTE BUNYAN.A. rejoined from C.R.S	
	5th			
	6th		—	
	7th			
	8th		Cpl POPPLE.H. 5853 with 3 men proceeded to HEILLY as advance party	
	9th		Left CARNOY 8.30 A.M. Arrive Heilly 12.30 P.M. PTE 704 TENNANT.J. 13077 BUNYAN.A. 897 PERRY.P. attached to NO32 M.V.S. for duty	
	10th	HEILLY	—	
	11th			
	12th		No2630 A/Sergt BISS W.J. transferred to No2 Vety Hosp. for transfer to Home Establishment	
	13th		21 Horses + 1 MULE to no 7 Vety Hosp.	
	14th		—	
	15th		—	
	16th		Orders received to take over from 29th M.V.S. position F.17.A.8.9 ALBERT sheet.	
	17th		—	
	18th		—	
	19th		—	
	20th		14 Horses 9 Mules to NO7. Vety Hosp	
	21st		Left HEILLY 9 A.M. arrived CARNOY 1 P.M. PTES TENNANT PERRY + BUNYAN rejoined	
	22nd		No14523 PTE BAMBER.R. + No11049 PTE YOXALL.H. arrived from 23rd Vety Hosp as Reinforcements	
	23rd		No4394 DAVIS.W. addt to 14th Corps Main Dressing Station	
	24th		44 Horses + 1 MULE transferred to NO7 VETY Hosp. No796 Sergt SEARS.T. arrived from No 6 Vety Hosp. in relief of No2630 A Sergt. BISS.W.J	
	25th			
	26th		—	
	27th		19 Horses to NO7 Vety Hosp.	
	28th			

A M Stewart Captain
OC 18th MVS

1577 Wt. W10791/1773 500,000 1/15 D. D. & L. A.D.S.S./Forms/C. 2118.

Vol 13

Confidential

War Diary

of

Capt C. M. Stewart

OC 18th M.V.S.

for Month of March 1917

Vol: Number X

Instructions regarding War Diaries and Intelligence Summaries are contained in F. S. Regs., Part II. and the Staff Manual respectively. Title pages will be prepared in manuscript.

WAR DIARY
or
INTELLIGENCE SUMMARY.
(Erase heading not required.)

Place	Date	Hour	Summary of Events and Information	Remarks and references to Appendices
CARNOY	1st		Orders received to proceed to HEILLY	
	2nd		—	
	3rd		22 Horses + 3 mules to No 7 V. H.	
	4th		Left CARNOY 9 A.M arrived HEILLY 1 P.M. took over No 19 BILLET	
HEILLY	5th			
	6th		7 Horses to No 7. V. H. No 3727 PTE. WEARING. H. + No 10341 PTE. ALMOND. F. arrived from No 1 V. H. as reinforcements	
	7th			
	8th		—	
	9th		—	
	10th		8 Horses to No 7 V. H.	
	11th		—	
	12th			
	13th			
	14th		PTE's MAHER. J. (2882) + PEPPER. E.W. (7050) rejoined from 32nd M. V. S.	
	15th		—	
	16th		—	
	17th		22 Horses + 10 Mules to No 7. V. H	
	18th		Orders received to proceed to OISSY on 20th.	
	19th			
	20th		Left HEILLY 8. A.M. arrived ARGOEUVES. 3 P.M. 19 Horses to No 7 V. H	
OISSY	21st		Left ARGOEUVES 9 AM arrived OISSY 1 P.M. Billet No 29.	
	22nd		—	
	23rd		20 Horses to ABBEVILLE by Road	
	24th		—	
	25th			
	26th		No 3727 PTE WEARING. to No 2 V. H being surplus to establishment	
	27th		—	
	28th		Orders received to proceed to VIGNACOURT 30th.	
	29th		5 Horses to ABBEVILLE by road	
	30th		Left OISSY 9 A.M. arrived VIGNACOURT 1 P.M.	
VIGNACOURT	31st		—	

Confidential

War Diary

of

Capt C. M. Stewart
OC 18th M. V. S.

For Month of April 1917

Volumn No. X

Vol 14

Army Form C. 2118.

Instructions regarding War Diaries and Intelligence Summaries are contained in F. S. Regs., Part II. and the Staff Manual respectively. Title pages will be prepared in manuscript.

WAR DIARY ~~or~~ of ~~INTELLIGENCE~~ SUMMARY.

(Erase heading not required.)

April 1917.

Place	Date	Hour	Summary of Events and Information	Remarks and references to Appendices
VIGNACOURT	1st.		Leave VIGNACOURT 10 A.M. arrive BEAUVAL 4 P.M.	
BEAUVAL	2nd		Leave BEAUVAL 9.30 A.M. arrive LUCHEUX. 1.30 P.M.	
LUCHEUX	3rd		15 Horses 1 Mule to 22 Vety Hospital	
	4th		19 " 4 " " " "	
	5th		Leave LUCHEUX 9 A.M. arrive BAVINCOURT. 130 P.M.	
BAVINCOURT	6th		No 704 PTE. TENNANT. J. transferred to No 5 General Base Depot on transfer to Cavalry.	
	7th		PTE No 29785 CUFF. A.J. attached from 2nd Bat. HANTS. Regt. No 17634 Sergt HARRISON. C. A.V.C. attached.	
	8th		–	
	9th		–	
	10th		Orders received to proceed to WAGNONLIEU on 12th.	
	11th			
	12th		Leave BAVINCOURT 9. A.M. orders received in route to proceed to AGNEZ arrived 2.30 PM	
AGNEZ	13th		Sergt HARRISON. A.V.C. dispatched to 92nd Bty R.F.A. for duty	
	14th		Took over from M.V.S. 12th Div. 22 O.R. attached as base conducting party	
	15th		No 1737 HILLIER T. No 5667 SWINBOURNE. R. No 515 THOMPSON W. to VII Corps mobile Vety Detachment.	
	16th			
	17th		88 Horses 2 MULES to No 22 Vety Hosp. No 5592 S.S. MUIR. R. arrived from 14 Vety Hosp	
	18th		87 " 4 Mules " " " " No 15062 S.S. FISH. W.H. to No 22 Vety Hosp	
	19th		–	
	20th		11 Horses 4 Mules to No 22 Vety Hosp	
	21st		11 " 4 " " " " " D.D.V.S. III rd ARMY visited section	
	22nd		–	
	23rd		–	
	24th		64 " 5 " " " " " "	
	25th		13 " 1 " " " " " "	

[signature] Captain
OC 18th M.V.S.

Army Form C. 2118.

Instructions regarding War Diaries and Intelligence Summaries are contained in F. S. Regs., Part II. and the Staff Manual respectively. Title pages will be prepared in manuscript.

WAR DIARY
or
INTELLIGENCE SUMMARY.
(Erase heading not required.)

Place	Date	Hour	Summary of Events and Information	Remarks and references to Appendices
AGNEZ	26th		3 Men returned from VI corps M.V. detachment	
	27th		No 18745 PTE COWBURN. R arrived from No 6 Vety Hosp. as reinforcement.	
	28th		220. R transferred to 11th M.V.S. 3rd Div. Leave AGNEZ 930 A.M. arrive LOUIN 3-30. PM.	
	29th		–	
	30th		–	

[signature] Captain
OC 11th M.V.S.

1577 Wt. W10791/1773 500,000 1/15 D. D. & L. A.D.S.S./Forms/C. 2118.

Vol 15

Confidential

War Diary

of

Captain C. M. Stewart

OC 18th M.V.S

From 1.5.17 To 31.5.17

Vol No X

Army Form C. 2118.

Instructions regarding War Diaries and Intelligence Summaries are contained in F. S. Regs., Part II. and the Staff Manual respectively. Title pages will be prepared in manuscript. MAY

WAR DIARY
or
~~INTELLIGENCE SUMMARY.~~

(Erase heading not required.)

Place	Date	Hour	Summary of Events and Information	Remarks and references to Appendices
COUIN	1st		orders received to proceed to ARRAS on 2nd. No 1782 PTE LAKE A. addt to C.C.S.	
	2nd		Left COUIN 9 A.M. arrived AGNEZ 3.30 P.M.	
	3rd		—	
	4th		—	
	5th			
	6th		21 Horses 7 Mules to No 22 Vety Hosp.	
	7th		1 NCO 9 O.R attached from 27th M.V.S. 15th Div.	
	8th		4 Horses 3 mules to No 22 V.H Pte CUFF (29785) returned to 2nd Hants Regt.	
	9th		—	
	10th		—	
	11th		3 Men to XI Corps M.V. detachment. No 24519 PTE WINCHESTER J. arrived from No 2 V.H	
	12th		—	
	13th		Orders received to proceed to ACHICOURT.	
	14th		5 Horses to No 22 V.H	
	15th			
	16th		Left AGNEZ 10 A.M arrived ACHICOURT 12.30 P.M	
	17th			
	18th		No 8576 PTE COOK W. arrived from No 4 V.H	
	19th		26 H 7 Mules to No 22 V.H.	
	20th		—	
	21st		39 H + 3 MULES to No 22 V.H	
	22nd			
	23rd		16 H 3 M. to No 22 V.H. No 1737 PTE HILLIER T. transferred to R.G.A depot Gosport.	
	24th			
	25th		—	
	26th		32 H + 6 M to No 22 V.H 1 N.C.O. 4 MEN returned to No 2 V.H.	
	27th			
	28th		14 H + 2 M. - - - - - - 1 Man returned to No 2 V.H	
	29th		—	
	30th		4 H + 2 Mules - - - - 2 Men	
	31st		Orders received to proceed to BERNAVILLE on the 2nd	[illegible] Captain OC 14th M.V.S.

1577 Wt. W10791/1773 500,000 1/15 D. D. & L. A.D.S.S./Forms/C. 2118.

Vol 16

War Diary

of

Capt. C. M. Stewart
of 18th M. V. S.

From 1-6-17 To 30-6-17

Vol: Number. X.

Instructions regarding War Diaries and Intelligence Summaries are contained in F. S. Regs., Part II. and the Staff Manual respectively. Title pages will be prepared in manuscript.

JUNE

WAR DIARY

or

~~INTELLIGENCE SUMMARY.~~

(Erase heading not required.)

Army Form C. 2118.

Place	Date	Hour	Summary of Events and Information	Remarks and references to Appendices
ACHICOURT.	1st		No 5286 PTE GANEL W. arrived from No4 Vety Hosp. as reinforcement	
	2nd		18 H's & 2 Mules to NO22 VETY HOSP. Left ACHICOURT 330 PM. arrived BERNEVILLE 530 PM	
	3rd		Left BERNEVILLE 7 AM. arrived LUCHEUX 130 PM.	
	4th		Left LUCHEUX 8 A.M. arrived BERNAVILLE	
	5th		—	
	6th		—	
	7th		—	
	8th		Inspection of Section by A.D.V.S. 29th Div.	
	9th		—	
	10th		NO8572 PTE COOK to Hospital	
	11th		CAPT. C.M. STEWART. proceeded on leave to PARIS.	
	12th		—	
	13th		—	
	14th		—	
	15th		CAPT C.M STEWART returned from leave	
	16th		—	
	17th		—	
	18th		P.A. Corpl Clarke G. (5238) to 87th Inf Bde as relief for Vety Sergt gone on leave.	
	19th		P.A Corpl Clarke G. (5238) promoted to P.A Sergt (Local corps order No65 dated 15.6.17)	
	20th		12 H's & 2 Mules to No 22 Vety Hosp.	
	21st		—	
	22nd		—	
	23rd		—	
	24th		Orders received to Entrain at DOULLENS 3·19 AM on 27th June	
	25th		15 H's 2 M's to No22. No796 SERGT. SEARS. to No24 Vety Hosp.	
	26th		Left BERNAVILLE 7 PM. to entrain at DOULLENS. ~~Entrained 1245 AM~~	
	27th		Entrained 1245 AM. arrived HOPOUTRE 11 AM. & proceeded to VOX-VRIE Farm took over billets from 49th M.V.S. situated A.9.C.7.3. sheet 28. Took over 16 Sick animals.	
	28th		—	
	29th		—	
	30th		—	

C.M. Stewart Captain
OC 18th M.V.S.

1577 Wt. W10791/1773 500,000 1/15 D. D. & L. A.D.S.S./Forms/C. 2118.

Confidential

July 1917

Vol 17

War Diary

of

No. 18. Mobile Vety Section

Volume No. 3

Instructions regarding War Diaries and Intelligence Summaries are contained in F. S. Regs., Part II. and the Staff Manual respectively. Title pages will be prepared in manuscript.

WAR DIARY of O.C. 18th M.V.S.
~~or~~
~~INTELLIGENCE SUMMARY.~~
(Erase heading not required.)

JULY.

Army Form C. 2118.

Place	Date	Hour	Summary of Events and Information	Remarks and references to Appendices
~~1st July~~ VOXVRIE FARM	1st July 2nd "		No 669 PTE HOLLAND + No 13077 PTE HOLLAND proceeded on leave (3rd to 13th)	
	3rd		A.D.V.S. XIV Corps visited section	
	4th		59 Horses 2 Mules to 23 V.H. by road.	
	5th		2 Horses to No 23 V.H by motor ambulance	
	6th		MAJOR. GEN. DE. LISLE KCB inspected section.	
	7th 8th		No 5562 Corpl Bryant 5286 PTE CANES 18745 PTE COWBURN to XIV Corps M.V.D	
	9th		No 5477 PTE. MASON to XIV Corps M.V.D D.A.D.V.S. visited Sect	
	10th		18 Horses 6 Mules to 23 V H by Road	
	11th		—	
	12th		1 Horse 1 Mule to No 23 V H by Motor ambulance	
	13th		—	
	14th 15th		PTE BUNYAN rejoins from leave 1 H 4 Mules to M.V.D 328 S.Sgt MANSBRIDGE A.W. joined section from No 1 V. Hosp. for duty.	
	16th		PTE HOLLAND rejoined from leave	
	17th		15 Mules 8 Horses to No 12 V Hosp by train No 5562 L Corpl Bryant promoted P.A. Corpl from 4th July 1917. Local Corps order 68 dated 12.7.17. No 10341 PTE ALMOND proceeded on leave to England 45 Horses 7 Mules to 23 V. Hosp by Road	
	18th		—	
	19th		2 Horses to No 23 V H by motor amb.	
	20th		orders received to move to Proven 21.7.17.	
	21st 22nd		Moved to PROVEN 10 sick animals handed over to 49th M.V.S.	
PROVEN.	23rd 24th		—	
	25th		No 2636 Sergt WILLIAMS proceeded on leave A.D.V.S. XIVth Corps inspected unit equipment	
	26th		—	
	27th		14 sick Horses to 13th V.H thro Corps M.V.D	
	28th		26 " " to 23 V.H. by Road No 2682 PTE MAHER J proceeded on leave to England	
	29th 30th		—	
	31st		9 " " to Corps M.V.D.	

[illegible] Captain
O.C. 18th M.V.S.

1577 Wt. W10791/1773 500,000 1/15 D. D. & L. A.D.S.S./Forms/C. 2118.

Confidential

War Diary

of

Capt: C M Stewart OC 18 M.V.S.

From 1.8.17 To 31.8.17

Volume No X

Instructions regarding War Diaries and Intelligence Summaries are contained in F. S. Regs., Part II. and the Staff Manual respectively. Title pages will be prepared in manuscript.

AUGUST

WAR DIARY

or

~~INTELLIGENCE SUMMARY.~~

(*Erase heading not required.*)

Army Form C. 2118.

Place	Date	Hour	Summary of Events and Information	Remarks and references to Appendices
PROVEN.	1st		A.D.V.S. XIV th Corps visited section	
	2nd		—	
	3rd		—	
	4th		—	
	5th		2636 P/A/ Sergt Williams G. returned from leave	
	6th		10 sick animals to XIV th Corps M.V.D. 29490 PTE LYNCH. T.F. joined as reinforcement	
	7th		6 " — " —	
	8th		Left PROVEN & took over from 46th M.V.S. at St. Sixte.	
St Sixte	9th		2682 PTE MAHER J. returned from leave 6 sick animals to M.V.D.	
	10th		12 sick animals to Corps M.V.D	
	11th		9 — — —	
	12th		16 — — — —	
	13th		10 — — — —	
	14th		26954 PTE CRATHERN. W. proceeded to Essex base depot Calais 10 sick to M.V.D. NO 5592	
	15th		S.S. MUIR. R. proceeded on leave	
	16th		18 sick animals to M.V.D	
	17th		19 — — —	
	"		23 — — — — — No13077 PTE BUNYAN. A. NO669 HOLLAND. C. NO11049 YOXALL H.	
	18th		T2 12749 Dr Grey E. wounded by Enemy bomb 3 Animals killed & 6 wounded	
	19th		11 sick animals to M.V.D.	
	20th		8 — — —	
	21st		6 — — —	
	22nd		No447. Pte ROBERTSON J.G. arrived as reinforcement 6 sick animals to Corps M.V.D	
	26th		11 animals to Corps M.V.D.	
	27th		A.D.V.S. XIV th Corps visited section	
	28th		17 sick animals to M.V.D.	
	29th		28 " — " — " NO5653 Corpl. POPPLE. H proceeded on leave	
	30th		Left ST SIXTE 10.30 arrived PROVEN 12 noon	
	31st		2 sick Horses to M.V.D. NO5592 S.S. MUIR returned from leave	

[signature] Captain
OC 18th M.V.S.

Confidential

Vol 15

War Diary

of

Captain C M Stewart
OC 18th MVS

from 1-9-17 to 30-9-17

Volume No X.

Instructions regarding War Diaries and Intelligence Summaries are contained in F. S. Regs., Part II. and the Staff Manual respectively. Title pages will be prepared in manuscript.

September

WAR DIARY
or
~~INTELLIGENCE SUMMARY.~~
(Erase heading not required.)

Army Form C. 2118.

Place	Date	Hour	Summary of Events and Information	Remarks and references to Appendices
PROVEN	1st		—	
	2nd		15 sick animals to C.M.V.D. No TT0809 Pte DAWES. C.C. + SE 24300 PTE GORDON A.A. No 309 PTE HARPER J. arrived from No 2 V.H as reinforcements.	
	3rd		nil	
	4th		7 sick animals to C.M.V.D.	
	5th		15 " " C.M.V.D.	
	8th		No 5592 S.S. MUIR admt to Hospital. No 5653 Corpl. POPPLE rejoined from leave	
	9th		No 5238 Sergt Clark proceeded on leave	
	10th		6 sick animals to C.M.V.D.	
	15th		7 "	
	17th		No 328 S. Sergt. MANSBRIDGE A.W. proceeded on leave.	
	19th		12 sick animals to C.M.V.D.	
	20th		No T4.044077 Dr. Heeler rejoined from leave. orders received to ~~relieve~~ relieve 46th M.V.S. on 22nd.	
	21st		23 sick animals to C.M.V.D	
	22nd		No 5238 Sergt Clark rejoined from leave. Left PROVEN 10AM arrived in camp 12 noon	
	23rd		16 sick animals to C.M.V.D.	
	24th		CAPT. C M STEWART. proceeded on leave T4.045319 Dr CAMPBELL arrived as reinforcement from A.S.C. Base depot.	
	25th		23 sick animals to C.M.V.D	
	26th		26 "	
	28th		16 " no 20300 S.S. BELL E arrived from No 12 V.H as reinforcement	
	29th		No 328 S. Sgt MANSBRIDGE rejoined from leave no. SE 14523 PTE Bamber R. proceeded on leave	
	30th		—	

C M Stewart Captain
OC 18th M.V.S.

Confidential

War Diary

of

Captain G. Gordon
OC 18th M V S

From 1.10.17. To 31.10.17.

Vol: No X.

Instructions regarding War Diaries and Intelligence Summaries are contained in F. S. Regs., Part II. and the Staff Manual respectively. Title pages will be prepared in manuscript.

OCTOBER.

WAR DIARY
or
~~INTELLIGENCE SUMMARY.~~
(Erase heading not required.)

Army Form C. 2118.

Place	Date	Hour	Summary of Events and Information	Remarks and references to Appendices
J Camp	1 10/17		22 Sick animals evacuated to C.M.V.D.	
" "	2 10/17		16 " " " " "	
" "	3 "			
" "	4 "		2 sick animals evacuated to C.M.V.D.	
" "	5 "		33 " " " " "	
" "	6 "		Leave J Camp 10 a.m., arrive Elverdinghe 12.30 p.m.	
" "	" "		Capt Stewart rejoined from leave in U.K.	
Elverdinghe	7 "			
"	8 "		18 sick animals to 46th M.V.S.	
"	9 "		14 " " " " " " "	
"	10 "		Received orders to proceed to Pardo Camp on 11 10/17	
"	11 "		Leave Elverdinghe 10 a.m. arrive Pardo Camp 12.30 p.m.	
Pardo Camp	12 "		No. 14523 Pte Bamber rejoined from leave in U.K.	
"	13 "		5 sick animals evacuated to C.M.V.D.	
"	14 "		Orders received to entrain at Peselhoek siding on 16 10/17	
"	15 "		Cpl Bryant C. Pte Cowburn. Pte Mason rejoined from C.M.V.D.	
"	16 "		Leave Pardo Camp 9 p.m. arrive Peselhoek siding 11.30 p.m. & camped there for night.	
"	17 "		Entrain Peselhoek siding 5.30 a.m., arrived [illegible] 10 p.m. marched to Bassenx	
Bassenx	18 "		~~arrived Bassenx~~ 1 a.m.	
"	19 "			
"	20 "			
"	21 "			
"	22 "		A.D.V.S. VI Corps inspected the section	
"	23 "			
"	24 "			
"	25 "		Capt. C.M. Stewart A.V.C. proceeded to No. 5 Vety Hospital, Abbeville.	
"	26 "		Capt. G. Gordon A.V.C. arrived	
"	27 "		8 horses & one mule transferred sick to No. 7 Vety Hospital	
"	28 "		No. 5286 Pte Game admitted to hospital	
"	29 "			
"	30 "			
"	31 "			

G. Gordon Capt A.V.C.
O.C. 18th M.V.S.

1577 Wt. W10791/1773 500,000 1/15 D. D. & L. A.D.S.S./Forms/C. 2118.

Vol 21

Confidential

War Diary

of

Captain G Gordon

OC 18th MVS

from 1-11-17 To 30-11-17

Vol: No X

Army Form C. 2118.

WAR DIARY

~~or~~

~~INTELLIGENCE SUMMARY.~~

(Erase heading not required.)

Instructions regarding War Diaries and Intelligence Summaries are contained in F. S. Regs., Part II. and the Staff Manual respectively. Title pages will be prepared in manuscript.

November

Place	Date	Hour	Summary of Events and Information	Remarks and references to Appendices
BASSEUX.	1st		Collect 38 Horses 1 Mule from 29th Div Artillery for Evacuation	
	2nd		No T4/045319 DR. Campbell ASC proceeds on Leave to Ireland.	
	3rd		47 Horses 1 Mule Evacuated to No 7 Vety Hospital	
	4th		Orders received from A.V.C. Base Records to despatch Category "A" men to No 2 Vety Hospital	
	5th		Collect 1 Sick Horse from Sarton, left with French Inhabitant	
	6th		6 Horses + 1 Mule transferred Sick to No 7 Vety Hospital	
	7th		No 515 Pte THOMPSON W. proceeds on Leave to ENGLAND	
	8th		Collect 1 Horse from Area Commandant SAULTY + Destroyed (Broken Leg)	
	9th		Finish Building Stables for Horses	
	10th		No 5562 Cpl Bufant C. proceeds on Leave to ENGLAND	
	11th		Nil	
	12th		Collect 6 Horses from AUTHIEULE for Evacuation to Vety Hospital	
	13th		13 Sick Animals to No 7 Vety Hospital. ADVS VI Corps visits Section	
	14th		Receive orders to move on the 16th 11.17. No 15745 Pte COWBURN R proceeds on Leave	
	15th		Leave Basseux 6 P.M. + march with Div H.Q. Transport Column	
BAPAUME	16th		Arrive BAPAUME 4 AM.	
	17th			
	18th		Leave BAPAUME 3.30 PM arrive MOISLAIN 9 PM.	
MOISLAIN	19th		No T4/045319 DR. CAMPBELL ASC Rejoins from Leave. Leave MOISLAIN 10.30 AM, arrive NURLU 1 PM.	
NURLU	20th		Leave NURLU 11 AM. arrive DESSART WOOD 2 PM. No 7053 Pte PEPPER AVC proceeds on Leave	
DESSART WOOD	21st		16 Sick Animals to IV Corps V.C.C.S. No 15260 Pte WILLIS AVC. arrives as Reinforcement	
	22nd		Nil	
	23rd		No 5667 Pte SWINBURN. R. proceeds on Leave to England.	
	24th		No. 16907 Pte Antliff, No. 16907 Pte Ashton. No 27650 Pte Coffin + No 12489 Pte Huxley. arrive from No 24 Vety Hospital to replace Category "A" men. 4 Sick Animals to IV Corps V.C.C.S.	
	25th		No 5981 Pte Crummett J. No 2653 Pte Maher, J. No 897 Pte Perry P. despatched to No 2 Vety Hospital for transfer to fighting units as Category "A". 6 Sick Animals to IV Corps V.C.C.S.	
	26th		No 515 Pte Thompson W. rejoins from Leave 6 Sick Animals to IV Corps V.C.C.S.	
	27th		4 Sick Animals to IV Corps V.C.C.S.	
	28th		Nil	
	29th		No 5562 Cpl Bufant rejoins from Leave	
	30th		Move Camp back to NURLU	

C. Gordon Capt AVC
OC 18 M.V.S.

T577. Wt. W10791/1773 500,000 1/15 D. D. & L. A.D.S.S./Forms/C. 2118.

18 Mob Vety Sec
Vol 22

Confidential

War Diary

of

Captain G Gordon
OC 18th MVS

from 1st.10.17 to 31.10.17

Vol No X

Instructions regarding War Diaries and Intelligence Summaries are contained in F. S. Regs., Part II. and the Staff Manual respectively. Title pages will be prepared in manuscript.

WAR DIARY
or
~~INTELLIGENCE SUMMARY.~~
(Erase heading not required.)

Army Form C. 2118.

December

Place	Date	Hour	Summary of Events and Information	Remarks and references to Appendices
NURLU	1.12.17.		Nil.	
	2.12.17.		12 Sick Animals to 14 Corps VECS.	
	3.12.17.		No 15745 Pte Cowburn R. Rejoins from leave	
	4.12.17.		35 Sick Animals to 14 Corps VECS. No 447 Pte Robertson proceeds on leave	
	5.12.17.		Leave Nurlu 10 AM. Arrive BAPAUME 6 PM.	
BAPAUME	6.12.17.		Leave Bapaume 8 AM arrive Courcelle 6 PM.	
Courcelle	7.12.17.		Leave Courcelle 10 AM arrive Le Cauroy 12.30 PM	
Le Cauroy	8.12.17.		Billet in Barn No 34. Officers Billet 74.	
	9.12.17.		" " "	
	10.12.17.		Collect 1 Mule from Inhabitant at WARLINCOURT.	
	11.12.17.		" " "	
	12.12.17.		No 9053 Pte Pepper Rejoins from leave	
	13.12.17.		DADVS proceeds on leave. OC MVS acting DADVS	
	14.12.17.		14 Sick Animals to No 14 Vety Hospital. No 5477 Pte Mason proceeds on leave	
	15.12.17.		" " "	
	16.12.17.		No 5508 Pte Simmons proceeds on leave	
	17.12.17.		Leave Le Cauroy 10 AM. Arrive Conchy-sur-Canche 6 PM.	
Conchy-sur-Canche	18.12.17.		Leave Conchy-sur-Canche 9 AM. arrive FRESSIN 6 PM.	
Fressin	19.12.17.		Leave Fressin 9 AM arrive Hucqueliers 10 PM. Billet in School Room	
	20.12.17.		Leave Hucqueliers 10 AM. Arrive PREURES 12 Noon. Billet in Farm	
PREURES	21.12.17.		No 309 Pte Harper W. awarded 28 Days No 1 FP for not complying with an order & Insolence	
	22.12.17.		No 5667 Pte Swinburn rejoins from leave & dispatched to No 2 Vety Hospital Havre as Category "A"	
	23.12.17.		No 447 Pte Robertson rejoins from leave	
	24.12.17.		" " "	
	25.12.17.		Church Parade at Hucqueliers for All Troops. Xmas Dinner in Farm House.	
	26.12.17.		" " " " "	
	27.12.17.		No 6474 & TT 0809 Ptes Munro & Dawes proceed on leave	
	28.12.17.		No 338 Sergt Marshall proceeds on 5 Days leave to ONS-EN-BRAY France	
	29.12.17.		DADVS returns from leave & visits Section	
	30.12.17.		No 541412 2nd Sapper Sales RE returned to his unit 497 HA Coy RE	
	31.12.17.		No 5477 Pte Mason R. [illegible] from leave No 5[illegible] Pte Gordon admitted to Hospital	

G. [illegible] Capt AVC
OC 18th [illegible] VS

1577 Wt. W10791/1773 500,000 1/15 D. D. & L. A.D.S.S./Forms/C. 2118.

Confidential

Vol 23

War Diary

of

Captain G Gordon

OC 18th M V S 29 Division

From 1.1.18 To 31.1.18

Volume No X

27

Instructions regarding War Diaries and Intelligence Summaries are contained in F. S. Regs., Part II. and the Staff Manual respectively. Title pages will be prepared in manuscript.

WAR DIARY
or
~~INTELLIGENCE SUMMARY.~~
(Erase heading not required.)

Army Form C. 2118.

January

Place	Date	Hour	Summary of Events and Information	Remarks and references to Appendices
PREURES	1-1-18		No 5508 Pte Simms rejoins from Leave	
	2-1-18		NIL	
FAUQUEMBERGUES	3-1-18		Leave PREURES 9-30 AM. arrive FAUQEMBERGUES 2 PM.	
WIZERNES	4-1-18		LEAVE FAUQUEMBERGUES 9AM. arrive WIZERNES 2 PM	
	5-1-18		Captain Gordon proceeds on Leave to U.K	
	6-1-18		NIL	
	7-1-18		10 Horses 2 Mules to No 23 Vety Hospital by Road	
	8-1-18		No 5562 Cpl Bryant & Ptes Ashton, Bamber, & Thompson to VIII Corps V.C.C.S for Duty	
			No. 6034 Pte Attwell rejoins from Leave.	
	9-1-18		No 20300 Pte Bell proceeds on Leave. 12 Horses to No 23 Vety Hospital by Road	
	10-1-18		NIL	
	11-1-18		Staff Sergeant Mansbridge to Calais for Remounts	
	12-1-18		6 Horses to No 23 Vety Hospital by Road. No. 0809 Pte Dawes & 5474 Pte Munro on Leave	
	13-1-18		Collect 3 Sick Horses from Inhabitant of Merck St. Lievin	
	14-1-18		No 15360 Pte Willis proceeds on Leave	
	15-1-18		6 Sick Animals to No 23 Vety Hospital by Road	
	16-1-18		No 24519 Pte Winchester proceeds on Leave	
ZIMERZEEL	17-1-18		Leave WIZERNES 9AM arrive ZIMERZEEL 3PM	
VLAMERTINGHE	18-1-18		Leave ZIMERZEEL 9AM arrive VLAMERTINGHE 2PM & take over Billets of 15th M.V.S	
	19-1-18		No 16907 Pte Ancliff proceeds on Leave	
	20-1-18		12 Horses 8 Mules to No 13 Vety Hospital by Road	
	21-1-18		No 5667 Pte Swinburn joins as reinforcement. Captain Gordon rejoins from Leave	
	22-1-18		No 5562 Cpl Bryant & 3 men rejoin from VIII Corps V.C.C.S	
	23-1-18			
	24-1-18			
	25-1-18			
	26-1-18		Pte Mc Leod joins as Reinforcement	
	27-1-18			
	28-1-18		Pte Mc Leod dispatched to No 23 Vety Hospital as Surplus 50 Sick Animals to No 23 Vety Hospital	
	29-1-18		No 13469 Pte Huxley proceeds on Leave. No 20300 S.S. Bell rejoins from Leave	
	30-1-18		ADVS visits Section	
	31-1-18		48 Sick Animals to No 13 Vety Hospital By Rail	

G Gordon
Captain
OC 18th M.V.S

1577 Wt. W10791/1773 500,000 1/15 D. D. & L. A.D.S.S./Forms/C. 2118.

Confidential

War Diary

of

Capt G Gordon

OC 18th Bn FS

From 1. 2. 18 To 28 2. 18

Volume No X

Instructions regarding War Diaries and Intelligence Summaries are contained in F. S. Regs., Part II. and the Staff Manual respectively. Title pages will be prepared in manuscript.

WAR DIARY
or
INTELLIGENCE SUMMARY.
(Erase heading not required.)

Army Form C. 2118.

February

Place	Date	Hour	Summary of Events and Information	Remarks and references to Appendices
Vlamertinghe	1-2-18		NIL	
	2-2-18		No 15360 Pte Wells Returns from Leave	
	3-2-18		No 314519 Pte Winchester Returns from Leave	
	4-2-18		32 Sick Animals to No 13 Vety Hospital by Rail	
	5-2-18		No 5663 Cpl H Popple despatched to No 2 Vety Hospital for training as Vety Sergt	
	6-2-18		NIL	
	7-2-18		35 Sick Animals to No 13 Vety Hospital by Rail. No 29490 Pte Lynch proceeds on Leave	
	8-2-18		No 16901 Pte Cantliff returns from Leave	
	9-2-18		NIL	
	10-2-18		NIL	
	11-2-18		44 Sick Animals to No 13 Vety Hospital by Rail	
	13-2-18		Leave Camp 11 AM. Arrive WATOU 3 PM. & take over Billets of 10th M.V.S	
	13-2-18		NIL	
	14-2-18		No 33061 Pte Ellamore joins as Reinforcement from No 2 Vety Hospital	
	15-2-18		No 12489 Pte Hurley Returns from Leave	
	16-2-18		NIL	
	17-2-18		NIL	
	18-2-18		NIL	
	19-2-18		NIL	
	20-2-18		NIL	
	21-2-18		8 Horses to No 13 Vety Hospital by Rail	
	22-2-18		NIL	
	23-2-18		DDVS Inspects Horses of MVS	
	24-2-18		NIL	
	25-2-18		31 Sick Animals to No 13 Vety Hospital by Rail	
	26-2-18		Building Stables	
	27-2-18		NIL	
	28-2-18		37 Sick Animals to No 13 Vety Hospital by Rail	

[signature] Capt. A.V.C.
O.C. 18th M.V.S.

Confidential

War Diary

of

Captain G. Gordon
OC 18th M.V.S.

From 1st. 3. 18 To 31. 3. 18

Volume No X

18

18 MVS
March
Vol 25

29

Instructions regarding War Diaries and Intelligence Summaries are contained in F. S. Regs., Part II. and the Staff Manual respectively. Title pages will be prepared in manuscript.

WAR DIARY
or
~~INTELLIGENCE SUMMARY.~~
(Erase heading not required.)

Army Form C. 2118.

March 1918.

Place	Date	Hour	Summary of Events and Information	Remarks and references to Appendices
Watou	1.3.18		Section being drilled by Infantry N.C.O.	
	2.3.18		— Ditto —	
	3.3.18		— Ditto	
	4.3.18		— Ditto —	
	5.3.18		— Ditto —	
	6.3.18		Orders Received to move on 7.3.18	
(S.28)	7.3.18		Leave WATOU 10 A.M. arrive at New Camp 1 P.M. Map position (S.28) G.8.b. 7.6	
G.8.b. 7.6.	8.3.18		17 Sick Animals by Rail to No 13. Vety Hospital	
	9.3.18		6 O.R. to VIII Corps. Vety: Evacuation Station for Duty	
	10.3.18		A.D.V.S. visits Station	
	11.3.18		Nil	
	12.3.18		Nil	
	13.3.18		N.C.O. to Calais for Remounts	
	14.3.18		36 Sick Animals to No 13 Vety Hospital	
	15.3.18		Nil	
	16.3.18		No 27650 Pte Coffin R. rejoins from Leave	
	17.3.18		Captain Gordon taken to Hospital. D.A.D.V.S. i/c 18th M.V.S.	
	18.3.18		No 28870 Pte Ashton proceeds on Leave to England	
	19.3.18		Nil	
	20.3.18		Nil	
	21.3.18		35 Sick Animals to No 13 Vety Hospital by Rail	
	22.3.18		Captain Gordon returns from Hospital	
	23.3.18		Nil.	
	24.3.18		17. Sick Animals to VIII Corps. Vety Evacuation Station	
	25.3.18		Nil	
	26.3.18		No 18745 Pte Cockburn R. Evacuated to C.C.S.	
	27.3.18		No 09440 Pte Fyner Evacuated to C.C.S. for X Ray treatment	
	28.3.18		14 Sick Animals to VIII Corps Vety E.S.	
	29.3.18		Nil	
	30.3.18		Nil	
	31.3.18			

R. Gordon Capt: A.V.C.
O.C. 18th M.V.S.

1577 Wt. W10791/1773 500,000 1/16 D. D. & L. A.D.S.S./Forms/C. 2118.

Confidential

War Diary

of

Capt G Gordon

OC 18th M V S

from 1st 4 18 To 30 4 18

Volume No X

Instructions regarding War Diaries and Intelligence Summaries are contained in F. S. Regs., Part II. and the Staff Manual respectively. Title pages will be prepared in manuscript.

WAR DIARY
or
~~INTELLIGENCE SUMMARY.~~
(Erase heading not required.)

Army Form C. 2118.

APRIL

Place	Date	Hour	Summary of Events and Information	Remarks and references to Appendices
G 5876	1-4-18		1 —	
Brandhoek	2-4-18		17 Sick Animals to VIII Corps Vety E.S.	
	3-4-18		11 " "	
	4-4-18		NIL	
	5-4-18		14 Sick Animals to VIII Corps Vety E.S	
	6-4-18		NIL	
	7-4-18		Receive orders to move 10.4.18	
	8-4-18		NIL	
	9-4-18		5 men Rejoin from VIII Corps Vety E.S 24 Sick Animals to VIII Corps Vety E.S.	
PONT LE PARC	10-4-18		Leave Camp at 7AM, & after waiting at FLETRE 8 hours arrive PONT. LE. PARC. 12 midnight	
	11-4-18		Leave PONT. LE PARC 2PM Arrive MORBEQUE 4 PM	
CASTRE	12-4-18		Reveille 3AM. Leave MORBEQUE 1PM Arrive CASTRE 3.30PM.	
St. SYLVESTRE CAPPEL	13-4-18		Leave Castre 8PM arrive Camp (Field on HAZEBROOK Rd) 10PM	
	14-4-18		Leave Camp 1PM arrive St SYLVESTRE CAPPEL 2PM. Billet in Farm	
	15-4-18		No 8315 Pte PLUMBLY arrives as Reinforcement from No 2 Vety Hospital	
	16-4-18		NIL	
	17-4-18		4 Sick Animals to XV Corps Vety E.S	
	18-4-18		ADVS XV Corps Visits Section	
HONDEGHEM	19-4-18		Leave SYLVESTRE CAPPEL 1.30 PM arrive HONDEGHEM 3 PM	
	20-4-18		3 Sick Animals to XV Corps Vety E.S	
	21-4-18		6 " "	
	22-4-18		No 27619 Pte HARRISON arrives from No 14 Vety Hospital	
	23-4-18		7 Sick Animals to XV Corps Vety E.S	
	24-4-18		9 " "	
	25-4-18		ADVS Visits Section	
	26-4-18		ADVS Visits Section	
	27-4-18		No 309 Pte HARPER Dispatched to No 2 Vety Hospital for transfer to Infantry	
STAPLE	28-4-18		Leave HONDEGHEM 10AM, Arrive STAPLE 1PM	
	29-4-18		9 Sick Animals to XV Corps Vety E.S Leave Staple 2PM arrive SERCUS 4.30 PM	
SERCUS	30-4-18		NIL	

G Gordon Capt AVC
OC 18th MVS

1577 W.W. 10791/1773 500,000 1/15 D. D. & L. A.D.S.S./Forms/C. 2118.

Confidential

War Diary

of

Capt: G. Gordon

OC 18th M.V.S.

from 1.5.18 to 31.5.18

Volumn No. X

WD 27

14

Instructions regarding War Diaries and Intelligence Summaries are contained in F. S. Regs., Part II. and the Staff Manual respectively. Title pages will be prepared in manuscript.

WAR DIARY
or
~~INTELLIGENCE SUMMARY.~~
(Erase heading not required.)

Army Form C. 2118.

May 1918

Place	Date	Hour	Summary of Events and Information	Remarks and references to Appendices
[illegible]	1.5.18		Nil	
	2.5.18		Ptes Ancliff Ashton Coppen Ellsmore Harrison & Huxley to XV Corps Vety E.S. for Duty	
	3.5.18		11 Sick Animals to XV Corps V.E.S.	
	4.5.18		Limbers & Wagons Repainted	
	5.5.18		Nil	
	6.5.18		War Establishment of MVS Reduced to 16 O.R. Authority A.G. 18.935.18 3.5.18	
	7.5.18		Nil	
	8.5.18		7 Sick animals to XV Corps V.E.S.	
	9.5.18		No 309 Pte Harper Rejoins from No 2 Vety Hospital	
	10.5.18		4 Sick Animals to XV Corps V.E.S.	
	11.5.18		No 21128 Pte EVANS & No 15010 Pte PHILLIPS join as Reinforcement from No 13 Vety Hospital	
	12.5.18		No 309 Pte HARPER W. dispatched to No 2 Vety Hospital as Surplus to Establishment	
	13.5.18		Nil	
	14.5.18		Nil	
	15.5.18		Aerial Torpedo drops on Billet of men, does not explode	
	16.5.18		Nil	
	17.5.18		Bombs fall in field adjoining Billet	
	18.5.18		12 Sick Animals to XV Corps Vety E.S.	
	19.5.18		No 8477 taken to Hospital, Sunstroke NYD	
	20.5.18		Nil	
	21.5.18		9 Sick Animals to XV Corps. Vety E.S.	
	22.5.18		Nil	
	23.5.18		Pte MASON Evacuated to 15th C.C.S.	
	24.5.18		11 Sick Animals to XV Corps Vety E.S.	
	25.5.18		Issue of Vety Stores to 29 Div units	
	26.5.18		Issue of Vety Stores to 29 Div units	
	27.5.18		Nil	
	28.5.18		Stray Animals admitted to MVS	
	29.5.18		Horse of Border Regt Dies of Suffocation (Gunshot Trachea)	
	30.5.18		Nil	
	31.5.18		Horse Hides dispatched to XV Corps V.E.S. & Vety Stores Boxes	

G. Gordon Capt. A.V.C.
OC 18th M.V.S.

1577 Wt. W10791/1773 500,000 1/15 D. D. & L. A.D.S.S./Forms/C. 2118.

Confidential

War Diary

of

Captain G GORDON

OC 18th M.G.S.

from 1.6.18 to 30.6.18

Volume No I

Army Form C. 2118.

WAR DIARY
or
~~INTELLIGENCE SUMMARY.~~
(Erase heading not required.)

Instructions regarding War Diaries and Intelligence Summaries are contained in F. S. Regs., Part II. and the Staff Manual respectively. Title pages will be prepared in manuscript.

June

Place	Date	Hour	Summary of Events and Information	Remarks and references to Appendices
SERCUS	1.6.18	..	NIL	
	2.6.18		3 Horses Transferred Sick to XV Corps V.E.S.	
	3.6.18		11 Animals Transferred Sick to XV Corps V.E.S.	
	4.6.18		NIL	
	5.6.18		13 Sick Animals to XV Corps V.E.S.	
	6.6.18		1 Stray Claimed by Australian F.A.	
	7.6.18		NIL	
	8.6.18		13 Sick Animals to XV Corps V.E.S. DDVS. visits Section	
	9.6.18		12 Sick Animals to XV Corps V.E.S.	
	10.6.18		1 Private attached from 1/3 Monmouth Regt for Tail Pulling in Div	
	11.6.18		NIL	
	12.6.18		No 565 Pte Morgan G.C. arrives as Reinforcement from No 3 Vety Hospital	
	13.6.18		ASC Dr Returned to No 1 Coy Train	
	14.6.18		8 Sick Animals to XV Corps V.E.S.	
	15.6.18		NIL	
	16.6.18		No 447 Cpl Robertson to Hospital suffering from fever	
	17.6.18		11 Sick Animals to XV Corps V.E.S. 2 Privates Sick with fever	
	18.6.18		3 more men Sick with fever	
	19.6.18		11. Sick Animals to XV Corps V.E.S.	
	20.6.18		Orders Received to move on the 22.6.18	
	21.6.18		7 Sick Animals to XV Corps V.E.S.	
Bandringham	22.6.18		Leave Sercus 10 AM. arrive Bandringham 2.PM.	
Wardrecques	23.6.18		Leave Bandringham 2 PM arrive WARDRECQUES 3.30 PM	
	24.6.18		No. 447 Cpl Robertson Rejoins from Hospital	
	25.6.18		NIL	
	26.6.18		NIL	
	27.6.18		2 Sick Animals by Road to No 23 Vety Hospital St Omer	
	28.6.18		NIL	
	29.6.18		NIL	
	30.6.18		Captain G Gordon proceeds on leave to ENGLAND. DADVS i/c 18th MVS	G Gordon Capt AVC ~~[illegible]~~ OC 18th M.V.S.

4

Instructions regarding War Diaries and Intelligence Summaries are contained in F. S. Regs., Part II. and the Staff Manual respectively. Title pages will be prepared in manuscript.

WAR DIARY
or
INTELLIGENCE SUMMARY.
(Erase heading not required.)

Army Form C. 2118. 29

18 Mob Vety Sec

VS 29

Place	Date	Hour	Summary of Events and Information	Remarks and references to Appendices
WARDRECQUES	1-7-18		3 Sick animals transferred to No 23 Vety Hospital	
	2-7-18		Nil	
	3-7-18		Nil	
	4-7-18		4 Horses transferred Sick to No 23 Vety Hospital	
	5-7-18		5 Sick Animals transferred Sick to " " "	
	6-7-18		6 Sick animals transferred Sick to " " "	
	7-7-18		Nil	
	8-7-18		5 Sick animals transferred Sick to No 23 Vety Hospital	
	9-7-18		Nil	
	10-7-18		10 Sick animals transferred Sick to No 23 Vety Hospital	
	11-7-18		64 Remounts arrive from Calais. 1 Mule Blk. G. collected from Mr Lefebvre Bandringham. Unit Unknown 1-6-18 to 11-7-18 days 41. 82 Francs.	
	12-7-18		Remounts issued to Units from M.V.S.	
	13-7-18		4 Sick animals transferred to No 23 Vety Hospital. 1 Horse hide	
	14-7-18		Corpl Bryant to 86th Bde for Duty	
	15-7-18		4 Sick animals transferred to No 23 Vety Hospital	
	16-7-18		Capt G Gordan Rejoins from Leave	
	17-7-18		1 H.D. Horse from Leinster Regt (Surplus) Issued to No 2 Coy 29th Div Train. 2 Horses from 86th Bde H.Q. (Surplus) 1. Horse from M.M. Police. Issued to 497 Kent Field Coy	
	18-7-18		6 Sick animals transferred sick to 23rd Vety Hospl.	
	19-7-18		1 L.D. Issued to 510th London Field Coy R.E. 1. Rider to 29th Div Machine Gun Corps (Surplus)	
	20-7-18		9 Sick animals transferred to No 23 Vety Hospital	
	21-7-18		orders received to move 22-7-18	
GYE?AERE	22-7-18		Leave Wardrecques 10 AM arrived GYE?AERE 3 PM Billet in Field	
	23-7-18		Nil	
	24-7-18		A.D.V.S. X Corps Visits Section	
	25-7-18		Collected 1 Horse from 92nd Battery 17th Bde R.F.A.	
	26-7-18		Nil	
	27-7-18		3 Sick animals transferred to X Corps V.E. Sations	
	28-7-18		3 Surplus Animals from Border Regt. Traffic Officers Pony Cured & Returned	
	29-7-18		3 Surplus Animals from Border Regt. Issued to 26th Battery 17th Bde RFA. 1 L.D. Issued to 1/2 Monmouth Regt. Captain Gordon acting D.A.D.V.S. Major Bowhay on leave.	
	30-7-18		4 Horses Transferred to X Corps V.E. Station. 1. Horse from No 3 Traffic Control Squadron. 1. Horse from 13th Battery R.F.A.	
	31-7-18		Sergt Williams proceeded on leave to U.K. 31-7-18	G. Gordon Capt AVC. OC 18th Mob. Vety. Sect.

1577 Wt. W10791/1773 500,000 1/15 D. D. & L. A.D.S.S./Forms/C. 2118.

Confidential

War Diary

of

Captain G. Gordon

OC 18th M V S

from 1st 8.18 to 31.8.18

Vol: No X

Army Form C. 2118.

Instructions regarding War Diaries and Intelligence Summaries are contained in F. S. Regs., Part II. and the Staff Manual respectively. Title pages will be prepared in manuscript.

WAR DIARY
~~or~~
~~INTELLIGENCE SUMMARY.~~
(Erase heading not required.)

Place	Date	Hour	Summary of Events and Information	Remarks and references to Appendices
1.8 18	1.8.18		4 Sick Animals to x Corps V.E.S	
BAVINCHOVE	2.8.18		Receive orders to move on 3rd to Billet U24.C.9.6	
U24.C.9.6	3.8.18		Leave Bavinchove 10.20 AM arrive U.24.C.9.6 1 PM	
	4.8.18		NIL	
	5.8.18		NIL	
	6.8.18		NIL	
	7.8.18		5 Sick Horses to XV Corps V.E.S.	
	8.8.18		NIL	
	9.8.18		NIL	
	10.8.18		2 Sick Horses to XV Corps V.E.S	
	11.8.18		NIL	
	12.8.18		2 Sick Horses to XV Corps V.E.S	
	13.8.18		7 Sick Horses to XV Corps V.E.S.	
	14.8.18		Capt Gordon A/DADVS Major Bowhay on leave	
	15.8.18		1 Horse to XV Corps V.E.S. Sergt Williams rejoins from leave	
	16.8.18		1 N.C.O. to Calais for Remounts	
	17.8.18		NIL	
	18.8.18		8 Sick Animals to XV Corps V.E.S.	
	19.8.18		Issuing Remounts from MVS arrived from Calais	
	20.8.18		Privates Scales, Charlton, Smith & Walker A.V.C. arrive from No 2 Vety Hospital to Replace Category "A" Men	
	21.8.18		Cpls Bryant & Robertson, Ptes Dawes & Simms despatched to No 2 Vety Hospital for Medical Inspection & transfer to Infantry	
	22.8.18		A.D.V.S. Visits Section	
	23.8.18		10 Remounts arrive 10 Sick Animals ~~.....~~ to XV Corps V.E.S.	
	24.8.18		Private Phillips proceeds on leave to ENGLAND	
	25.8.18		9 Sick Animals to XV Corps V.E.S. 2 Horses sent to 2 Army HQ Remount Section	
	26.8.18		Move Camp to U.24.a.5.6 on account of Light Railway being laid thro' Camp	
	27.8.18		31st Div Horse Show	
	28.8.18		3 Sick Animals to XV Corps V.E.S	
	29.8.18		Collect 1 Horse by Float from 28th A.F.A	
	30.8.18		3 Sick Animals to XV Corps V.E.S	
	31.8.18		Collect 1 Sick Horse from Machine Gun Coy by Float	

G. Gordon Capt A.V.C.
OC 18th M.V.S.

Confidential

War Diary

of

Capt. G. Gordon

O.C. 18th M.V.S.

From 1-9-18

To 30-9-18

Vol. No. X.

Instructions regarding War Diaries and Intelligence Summaries are contained in F. S. Regs., Part II. and the Staff Manual respectively. Title pages will be prepared in manuscript.

WAR DIARY
~~or~~
~~INTELLIGENCE SUMMARY.~~
(Erase heading not required.)

September 1918

1

Army Form C. 2118.

Place	Date	Hour	Summary of Events and Information	Remarks and references to Appendices
~~[illegible]~~	1.9.18		8 Sick Animals to C.V.E.S	
V34.a.5.6	2.9.18		NIL	
Nr WALLON-CAPPEL	3.9.18		Leave Camp 10 AM arrive HAZEBROUCK 12 noon. Map position V32.b.3.4.	
	4.9.18		1 NCO to Calais for Remounts	
	5.9.18		4 Sick Animals to XV Corps V.E.S	
	6.9.18		Received Orders to move to 27/W34.a.4.6. 60 Remounts arrive at M.V.S	
	7.9.18		XV Corps V.E.S take over Camp of M.V.S. 4 Sick Animals to V.E.S.	
27/W34.b.3.4	8.9.18		Move Camp to 27/W34 B.3.4.	
	9.9.18		NIL	
	10.9.18		Receive orders to move back to HAZEBROUCK on 11.9.18	
HAZEBROUCK	11.9.18		Leave Camp 2 PM arrive HAZEBROUCK 5 PM.	
	12.9.18		7 Sick Animals to XV Corps V.E.S	
	13.9.18		18 Horses Gassed admitted to M.V.S	
	14.9.18		19 Sick Animals to XV Corps V.E.S	
	15.9.18		NIL	
	16.9.18		1 Mule Collected from Inhabitant left by 31st D.A.C	
	17.9.18		10 Horses Sick to ~~XV~~ Corps V.E.S	
27/F22.b.5.5	18.9.18		Leave Camp 9-30 AM arrive New Camp 4.30 PM 27/F22.b.5.5	
	19.9.18		Digging Revetting around Horses against Bombs	
	20.9.18		A.D.V.S. II Corps visits Section for Inspection	
	21.9.18		7 Sick Animals to II Corps Vety E.S	

A7092 Wt. W125.9/M1293 750,000. 1/17. D. D & I. Ltd. Forms/C2118/14.

Instructions regarding War Diaries and Intelligence Summaries are contained in F. S. Regs., Part II. and the Staff Manual respectively. Title pages will be prepared in manuscript.

September 1918

WAR DIARY
or
~~INTELLIGENCE~~ SUMMARY.
(Erase heading not required.)

2

Army Form C. 2118.

Place	Date	Hour	Summary of Events and Information	Remarks and references to Appendices
27/F.22.b.55	22.9/18		Horses of [illegible] V.S. fetching Ammunition	
			Collect 1 mule Stray from Town Major WATOU	
	23.9.18			
	24.9.18		1 mule to II Corps V.E.S.	
	25.9.18		NIL	
	26.9.18		12 Sick Animals to II Corps V.E.S	
Brown FARM.	27.9.18		Leave Camp 2PM arrive Brandhoek 4.30 Brown Farm	
28/H11a.0.9.	28.9.18		4 Sick Animals to II Corps V.E.S. 3 men to advanced Post on Vlamertinghe-Ypres Rd	
	29.9.18		13 Sick Animals to II Corps V.E.S	
	30.9.18		55 Sick & wounded Animals to II V.E.S	

G. Gordon Capt A.V.C.
OC 18th M.V.S

A7092 Wt. W125.9/M1293 750,000. 1/17. D. D & L. Ltd. Forms/C2118/14.

Confidential

War Diary

of

Capt G. Gordon

OC 18th M.V.S.

From 1.10.18 to 31.10.18

Vol No X

Sheet 1

Instructions regarding War Diaries and Intelligence Summaries are contained in F. S. Regs., Part II. and the Staff Manual respectively. Title pages will be prepared in manuscript.

WAR DIARY
or
~~INTELLIGENCE SUMMARY.~~
(Erase heading not required.)

October 1918

Army Form C. 2118.

Place	Date	Hour	Summary of Events and Information	Remarks and references to Appendices
Ypres Vlamertinghe Rd.	1.10	18	3 OR to Advanced Post on Ypres Menin Rd 11 Sick Animals to 50th M.V.S.	
	2.10	18	14 Sick Animals to 50th M.V.S.	
	3.10	18	4 — — —	
	4.10	18	8 Sick Animals to 50th M.V.S. DR HEELER Returns from leave	
	5.10	18	11 Sick Animals to 50th M.V.S.	
	6.10	18	19 Sick Animals to 50th M.V.S.	
	7.10	18	Sergt CLARKE AVC proceeds on leave to England 7 Sick Animals to 50 M.V.S.	
	8.10	18	73 Remounts handed over to 18 M.V.S. for Issue	
	9.10	18	19 Sick Animals to 50th M.V.S.	
	10.10	18	DR ALLAN ASC proceeds on leave to UK 8 Sick Animals to 50th M.V.S.	
	11.10	18	Leave Camp on Ypres Vlamertinghe Rd & take over Camp on Ypres Menin Rd 7 Sick Animals to 50 M.V.S.	
Ypres. Menin Rd	12.10	18	7 Sick Animals to 50 M.V.S.	
	13.10	18	60 Remounts handed over to 18 M.V.S. for Issue	
	14.10	18	11 Sick Animals to 50 M.V.S. A.D.V.S. II Corps visits Section	
	15.10	18	Leave Camp 10 AM arrive Camp near BEČELAERE 2 PM 11 Sick Animals to 50 M.V.S.	
BECELAERE	16.10	18	Leave Camp 10 AM. arrive Camp Near DADIZEELE Rd. 3 PM. 5 Sick Animals to 50th M.V.S.	
DADIZEELE	17.10	18	Leave Camp 9 AM arrive LEDEGHEM 2 PM 5 Sick Animals to 50th M.V.S.	
LEDEGHEM.	18.10	18	A.D.V.S. visits Section (Second Corps)	
	19.10	18	6 Sick Animals to 50 M.V.S. 1 German Horse admitted	
	20.10	18	70 Remounts arrive at M.V.S. for Issue. 33 Sick Animals to 50th M.V.S. Leave Ledeghem 2 PM. arrive STEENBEEK 4 PM.	
STEENBEEK	21.10	18	No 30300 S.S. Bell admitted to Hospital 1 S.Smith attached from Div. Train	

A7092 Wt. W125.9/M1293 750,000. 1/17. D. D & L. Ltd. Forms/C2118/14.

Instructions regarding War Diaries and Intelligence Summaries are contained in F. S. Regs., Part II. and the Staff Manual respectively. Title pages will be prepared in manuscript.

Sheet 2

October

WAR DIARY
or
~~INTELLIGENCE~~ ~~SUMMARY.~~

(Erase heading not required.)

Army Form C. 2118.

Place	Date	Hour	Summary of Events and Information	Remarks and references to Appendices
Steenbeek	22 11 18		Leave Steenbeek 9 AM. arrive (29/H14 C34) Cuerne - Courtrai Rd. 4 PM. 7 Sick Animals to 50 M.V.S.	
29/H14 C34.	23-11-18		11 Sick Animals to 50 M.V.S.	
	24-10-18		Pte Smith A.S.C. proceeds on leave to U.K. 10 Sick Animals to 50 M.V.S.	
	25 10 18		4 Sick Animals to 50 M.V.S.	
	26 10 18		11 Sick Animals to 50 M.V.S. 5 Remount Mules arrive at M.V.S.	
	27-10 18		Leave Camp 8 Am. arrive MOUVAUX 4 PM. (15th Corps)	
MOUVAUX.	28 10 18		Sergt Clarke A.S.C. Returns from Leave	
	29-10 18		10 Sick Animals to 15th Corps V.R.S.	
	30 10 18		2 Mules Collected from Inhabitant at WASQUEHAL	
	31-10 18		Pte ALLAN A.S.C. Returns from leave 8 Sick Animals to 15th Corps V.R.S.	

G Gordon Capt A.V.C
O.C. 15th M.V.S.

A7092 Wt. W128 9/M1293 750,000. 1/17. D. D & L. Ltd. Forms/C2118/14.

Confidential

War Diary

of

Capt. G. Gordon

OC 18th M.V.S.

from 1st 11-18 to 30-11-18

Vol No X.

Instructions regarding War Diaries and Intelligence Summaries are contained in F. S. Regs., Part II. and the Staff Manual respectively. Title pages will be prepared in manuscript.

WAR DIARY
~~or~~
~~INTELLIGENCE~~ SUMMARY.
(*Erase heading not required.*)

Sheet I

Army Form C. 2118.

November

Place	Date	Hour	Summary of Events and Information	Remarks and references to Appendices
MOUVAUX	1·11·18		Pte 8315 Plumbly proceeds on leave to UK	
	2·11·18		16543 S.S. Saward joins unit as Reinforcement	
	3·11·18		7 Sick animals to 15th Corps V.E.S.	
	4·11·18		14523 Pte Bamber proceeds on leave to UK	
	5·11·18		5 Sick Animals to 15 Corps. V.E.S.	
	6·11·18		Nil	
	7·11·18		Leave Mouvaux 9AM arrive ROLLEGHEM 12 Noon 7 Sick Animals to 10th Corps V.E.S.	
Rolleghem	8·11·18		Nil	
	9·11·18		ADVS visits Section	
	10·11·18		Leave Rolleghem 10AM arrive St Genoa 2PM	
ST GENOA	11·11·18		Remain in Billets awaiting orders.	
	12·11·18		Nil	
	13·11·18		Leave St Genoa 11AM. arrive at Billet on RENAIX Rd. 5PM	
	14·11·18		Leave Billet 11AM arrive HORBECQ 4 PM	
Horbecq	15·11·18		28460 Pte Smith Returns from leave	
	16·11·18		31 Sick Animals to 40 M.V.S.	
	17·11·18		Received orders to move 18·11·18	
	18·11·18		30 Sick Animals to 11 Corps V.E.S.	
			Leave Horbecq 8·30AM arrive ENGHIEN 3PM.	
ENGHIEN	19·11·18		Destroy 1 HD Horse at Billet unable to move.	
	20·11·18		Leave ENGHIEN 10AM Arrive TUBECQ 5 PM.	
TUBECQ	21·11·18		8315 Pte Plumbly P returns from leave.	
	22·11·18		Leave Tubecq 9AM arrive Braine l' Alleud 5 PM.	
Braine-l-Alleud	23·11·18		Nil	
	24·11·18		Leave Braine-l-Alleud 10AM arrive OTTIGNIES 3PM	

A7092 Wt. W128 9/M1293 750,000. 1/17. D. D. & L. Ltd. Forms/C2118/14.

Instructions regarding War Diaries and Intelligence Summaries are contained in F. S. Regs., Part II. and the Staff Manual respectively. Title pages will be prepared in manuscript.

WAR DIARY
or
~~INTELLIGENCE~~ SUMMARY.
(Erase heading not required.)

Army Form C. 2118.

Sheet 2

November

Place	Date	Hour	Summary of Events and Information	Remarks and references to Appendices
OTTIGNES	25 11-18		515 Pte THOMPSON proceeds on leave	
	26 11-18		Leave Ottignes 12 noon arrive NIL ABBESSE 4 PM.	
NIL.ABBESSE	27-11-18		14523 Pte Bamber Rejoins from leave	
			Leave NIL.ABBESSE arrive GRAND.ROSIER 3PM.	
GRAND.ROSIER	28 11-18		Leave Grand.Rosier 10AM. arrive HUY 5 30 PM	
HUY	29 11 18		NIL	
	30 11 18		Leave HUY 10AM arrive ANTHIENES 4 30 PM	

[signature] Capt RE
OC 18 M.S.S.

Confidential

War Diary

of

Capt Gordon RAVC
OC 18th M.V.S.

from 1-10-18 to 31-10-18

Vol no. X.

December 1918 — 1

WAR DIARY
~~or~~
~~INTELLIGENCE SUMMARY.~~
(Erase heading not required.)

Army Form C. 2118.

Instructions regarding War Diaries and Intelligence Summaries are contained in F. S. Regs., Part II. and the Staff Manual respectively. Title pages will be prepared in manuscript.

Place	Date	Hour	Summary of Events and Information	Remarks and references to Appendices
ANTHISNES	1-12-18		Leave ANTHISNES 10 AM. Arrive SPIRMONT 3 PM.	
	2-12-18		Leave SPIRMONT 9 AM arrive NIVERRE 4 PM.	
NIVERRE	3-12-18		Nil	
Malmedy	4-12-18		Leave NIVERRE 9 AM arrive MALMEDY 4 PM	
Kalter Herberg	5-12-18		Leave Malmedy 8.30 AM arrive KALTER HERBERG 3.30 PM	
	6-12-18		Leave Kalter Herberg 8.30 AM arrive STREKENBORN 3.30 PM.	
Strekenborn	7-12-18		Leave Strekenborn 8.30 AM arrive ZULPICH 4 PM	
ZULPICH	8-12-18		~~Leave~~ Nil	
Efferen	9-12-18		Leave Zulpich 8.30 AM Arrive EFFEREN 3 PM.	
	10-12-18		Stay at Efferen for 76 Remounts from St Omer	
	11-12-18		Men from RA & Infantry attached with Sick Animals for the march	
	12-12-18		Nil	
	13-12-18		Leave Efferen 11 AM & march thro: Cologne & inspected by General on Rhine Bridge & arrive at Bensberg 5 PM	
Bensberg	14-12-18		Nil	
	15-12-18		Nil	
	16-12-18		ADVS 3 Corps visits Section	
	17-12-18		RA: personnel Returned to unit	
	18-12-18		Nil	
	19-12-18		5 men arrive from No 2 VES as Reinforcement for Sick Animals Privates Clifford, Cope, Kirkland, Pennington & Stevens	
	20-12-18		5 men Returned to Infantry units	
	21-12-18		Leave BENSBERG 11 AM Arrive N.W outskirts of BERG GLADBACH	

A7092 Wt. W128 9/M1293 750,000. 1/17. D. D & L. Ltd. Forms/C2118/14.

Army Form C. 2118.

WAR DIARY
or
~~INTELLIGENCE~~ SUMMARY.
(Erase heading not required.)

Instructions regarding War Diaries and Intelligence Summaries are contained in F. S. Regs., Part II, and the Staff Manual respectively. Title pages will be prepared in manuscript.

December 1918

Place	Date	Hour	Summary of Events and Information	Remarks and references to Appendices
BERG GLADBACH	22.12.18		Cleaning up Billets for Xmas & Building Tables & Mess Room etc	
	23.12.18		NIL	
	24.12.18		Leave Billet as not suitable & proceed to SE side of BERG GLADBACH 3 PM	
	25.12.18		Privates Thompson & Campbell Rejoin from Leave	
	26.12.18		Men have Dinner & Tea in Camp Amusements in Evening	
	27.12.18		No 7053 Cpl Pepper Rejoin from Leave	
	28.12.18		NIL	
	29.12.18		60 Sick Animals for Evacuation	
	30.12.18		NIL	
	31.12.18		NIL	

G. Gordon
Capt RAVC
OC 18th M.V.S.

18th MOBILE VETERINARY SECTION.
No. ....
Date 2.1.19.

A7092 Wt. W128.9/M1293 750,000. 1/17. D. D & L. Ltd. Forms/C2118/14.

Confidential

War Diary

of

Capt G Gordon

OC 18th MGS

from 1-1-19 to 31-1-19

Vol no X

Vol 36

Instructions regarding War Diaries and Intelligence Summaries are contained in F. S. Regs., Part II. and the Staff Manual respectively. Title pages will be prepared in manuscript.

WAR DIARY
or
~~INTELLIGENCE SUMMARY.~~
(Erase heading not required.)

Army Form C. 2118.

January 1919

Place	Date	Hour	Summary of Events and Information	Remarks and references to Appendices
Berg Gladbach	1-1-19		Nil 1 officer 16 OR attached for Vets Course	
	2-1-19		Pte Attwell proceeds on leave to England for 14 Days	
	3-1-19		DADVS & OC 18 MVS Classifying Animals in the Division	
	4-1-19		Nil	
	5-1-19		13 Sick Animals to Berg Gladbach Station for transfer to Base	
	6-1-19		No T4/044077 Dr Heller ASC despatched for Demobilization as Miner	
	7-1-19		56 Sick Animals by Road to No 3 VES at MULHEIM	
	8-1-19		Surplus Animals sent in to MVS by Div Units	
	9-1-19		Nil	
	10-1-19		17 Sick Animals to No 3 VES	
	11-1-19		Nil	
	12-1-19		Classification of Section Horses by DADVS	
	13-1-19		Pte 5474 Munro AVC proceeded on leave to England (14 days)	
	14-1-19		1 attached man despatched to Unit for Demobilization	
	15-1-19		No 5667 Pte Cranburn Returns from leave	
	16-1-19		Nil	
	17-1-19		Nil	
	18-1-19		Class "D" Horses sold to Butcher in Berg Gladbach (5 in number)	
	19-1-19		REs start building Stables for MVS	
	20-1-19		Class "D" Horses Sold to Butcher in Berg Gladbach (6 in number)	
	21-1-19		Nil	
	22-1-19		Nil	
	23-1-19		Nil	
	24-1-19		MVS Inspected by Major General Cayley GOC 29 Div	
	25-1-19		5034 Pte Attwell Returns from leave	
	26-1-19		Nil	
	27-1-19		Class "D" Horses sold to Butcher in Berg Gladbach (8 in number)	
	28-1-19		30 Class "D" Horses despatched to No 2 VES	
	29-1-19		ADVS visits Section	
	30-1-19		3 Mange Cases to No 3 VES	
	31-1-19		Nil	

G Gordon Capt RAVC
OC 18th MVS

A6091 Wt. W128 g/M1293 750,000. 1/17. D. D & L. Ltd. Forms/C2118/14.

18th M.V.S.
Duplicate
February

WAR DIARY
or
INTELLIGENCE SUMMARY.
(Erase heading not required.)

Army Form C. 2118.

Instructions regarding War Diaries and Intelligence Summaries are contained in F. S. Regs., Part II. and the Staff Manual respectively. Title pages will be prepared in manuscript.

Place	Date	Hour	Summary of Events and Information	Remarks and references to Appendices
Berg Gladbach	1.2.19		20 Class D Horses to No 2 VES for Destruction	
	2.2.19		Nil	
	3.2.19		10 OR attended for second [illegible] course of instruction	
	4.2.19		16 Class D Horses to No 2 VES for Destruction	
	5.2.19		1 Horse (open joint) sold to local butcher in Berg Gladbach	
	6.2.19		Nil	
	7.2.19		13 Sick Animals to No 2 VES	
	8.2.19		17 Sick Animals to No 2 VES	
	9.2.19		Horses reclassified by ADVS [illegible] to Unit	
	10.2.19		Nil	
	11.2.19		Private [illegible] Rejoined from leave	
	12.2.19		DADVS [illegible] 18 MVS. [illegible]	
	13.2.19		[illegible]	
	14.2.19		Nil	
	15.2.19		Nil	
	16.2.19		Animals reclassified by DDVS [illegible] for [illegible]	
	17.2.19		[illegible]	
	18.2.19		Nil	
	19.2.19		Section Horses [illegible] by Col. [illegible]	
	20.2.19		Private [illegible] Rejoined from leave	
	21.2.19		Nil	
	22.2.19		Section Horses malleined by OC [illegible]	
	23.2.19		Nil	
	24.2.19		14 Class "D" Animals to Slaughter House Berg Gladbach	
	25.2.19		13 Sick Animals to No 2 VES [illegible]	
	26.2.19		3 Horses cured & returned to Units	
	27.2.19		Nil	
	28.2.19		Nil	

C Gordon Capt.
OC 18th MVS

A7092 Wt. W125 9/M1293 750,000. 1/17. D. D & L. Ltd. Forms/C2118/14.

Vol 36

Confidential

War Diary

of

Capt G. Goran

OC 18th [illegible]

from 1-3-19 to 31-3-19

Vol No. X.

22

WAR DIARY
or
~~INTELLIGENCE~~ SUMMARY.
(Erase heading not required.)

Army Form C. 2118.

Instructions regarding War Diaries and Intelligence Summaries are contained in F. S. Regs., Part II. and the Staff Manual respectively. Title pages will be prepared in manuscript.

March 1919

Place	Date	Hour	Summary of Events and Information	Remarks and references to Appendices
Berg Gladbach	1-3-19		NIL	
	2-3-19		NIL	
	3-3-19		14 Sick Animals to No 2 VES Mulheim	
	4-3-19		1 Private Evacuated to Hospital (Sick) 5 Cases for Butcher	
	5-3-19		[illegible] proceeds on leave to UK OC 18th M.V.S. [illegible]	
	6-3-19		1 Horse sold to Butcher in Berg Gladbach	
	7-3-19		Pte Walker Rejoins from leave	
	8-3-19		Sgt Clarke to Cologne with 7 Horses for Vety work	
	9-3-19		NIL	
	10-3-19		12 Sick Animals to No 2 VES Mulheim 9 Cases for Butcher	
	11-3-19		NIL	
	12-3-19		Vety Stores arrive & are distributed to Divl Units	
	13-3-19		NIL	
	14-3-19		11 Sick Animals to No 2 VES Mulheim	
	15-3-19		1 Horse collected by Float from House at DINWALD	
	16-3-19		NIL	
	17-3-19		At Point to Point Races Horse Ambulance in Attendance	
	18-3-19		34 Sick Animals to No 2 VES 20 Cases for Butcher included	
	19-3-19		11 Sick Animals to No 2 VES 10 Cases for Butcher included	
	20-3-19		Nil	
	21-3-19		Nil	
	22-3-19		All Surplus Wagons to be Returned to Area Commandant	
	23-3-19		Nil	
	24-3-19		Charger from 57 Bde HQ to be Retained for Treatment	
	25-3-19		1 Horse from Leinster Regt in exchange for Section Horse (Sick)	
	26-3-19		Pte Morgan RAVC proceeds on leave to UK	
	27-3-19		17 Sick Animals to No 2 VES, 2 Animals to Butcher Berg Gladbach	
	28-3-19		32 Sick Animals to No 2 VES for Destruction. No 3738 Sergt Clarke Demobilized	
	29-3-19		11 Sick Animals to No 2 VES for Destruction	
	30-3-19		Surplus & Spinks Wagon to Area Commandant Berg Gladbach	
	31-3-19		NIL	

C. Gordon Capt RAVC
OC 18th M.V.S.

18th MOBILE VETERINARY SECTION.
No.
Date 1-4-19

A7092 Wt. W123 9/M1293 750,000. 1/17. D. D & L Ltd. Forms/C2118/14.

Instructions regarding War Diaries and Intelligence Summaries are contained in F. S. Regs., Part II. and the Staff Manual respectively. Title pages will be prepared in manuscript.

WAR DIARY
or
INTELLIGENCE SUMMARY.
(Erase heading not required.)

Army Form C. 2118.

April 1919.

Place	Date	Hour	Summary of Events and Information	Remarks and references to Appendices
Berg. Gladbach	1.4.19		Sick Horse sold to Butcher in Berg Gladbach for slaughter	
	2.4.19		No. 27437 Pte Haycock. RAVC. arrives as Reinforcement to unit	
	3.4.19		Nil	
	4.4.19		Nil	
	5.4.19		No 7052 Cpl Pepper RAVC. & No 12646 Pte Chadwin for Demobilization	
	6.4.19		Privates Gray, Cammels & Strand arrive as Reinforcements to unit	
	7.4.19		17 Sick animals sent to No 2 VES.	
	8.4.19		1 Sick Horse sold to Butcher Berg Gladbach for slaughter	
	9.4.19		Nil	
	10.4.19		1 Horse sick sold to Butcher Berg Gladbach for slaughter	
	11.4.19		Nil	
	12.4.19		No 5667 Pte Swinburne Demobilized. Capt Hill RAVC. take over charge of 18 MVS	
	13.4.19		No 20681 Pte Tinch arrives as Reinforcement to Section	
	14.4.19		Sgt Richardson RAVC. Attached for Duty with 18 MVS	
	15.4.19		565 Pte Morgan Rejoins from Leave	
	16.4.19		565 Pte Morgan & 8315 Pte Plumbley RAVC Demobilized	
	17.4.19		ADVS. visits 18 MVS for inspection of unit	
	18.4.19		Nil	
	19.4.19		5 Sick Animals to No 2 VES	
	20.4.19		Nil	
	21.4.19		1 Horse Issued to V.O. 46 DAC.	
	22.4.19		1 Horse Sick Sold to Butcher in Berg Gladbach for slaughter	
	23.4.19		No TT/01507 Pte Walker arrives as Reinforcement to unit	
	24.4.19		No 31488 Pte Payne & No 30909 Pte Riddell RAVC join as Reinforcement to unit	
	25.4.19		2 Sick Horses to No 2 VES.	
	26.4.19		Nil	
	27.4.19		Nil	
	28.4.19		Nil	
	30.4.19.		Privates Eccles Munro & Winchester RAVC Despatched for Demobilization	
	30.4.19.		1 Mange Case to No 2 VES.	J. Hill Capt RAVC O.C. 18 MVS

A7092 Wt. W4253/M1293 750,000 1/17. D. D. & L. Ltd. Forms/C2118/14.

Confidential

25

War Diary

of

Capt Hill

OC 18th MVS

from 1-5-19

To 31-5-19

Vol: No X

Army Form C. 2118.

Instructions regarding War Diaries and Intelligence Summaries are contained in F. S. Regs., Part II. and the Staff Manual respectively. Title pages will be prepared in manuscript.

WAR DIARY

or

~~INTELLIGENCE SUMMARY.~~

(Erase heading not required.)

May 1919.

Place	Date	Hour	Summary of Events and Information	Remarks and references to Appendices
Berg Gladbach	1.5.19		Nil	
	2.5.19		Nil	
	3.5.19		1 Stray mule found & claimed by Devon Regt	
	4.5.19		1 OR proceeds on leave to England	
	5.5.19		German civilian putting feeding troughs in stables	
	6.5.19		Received 2 Horses of Capt [illegible] (Deceased)	
	7.5.19		1 mule sold to Butcher for consumption Amount realised 663 MKS	
	8.5.19		2 Men (R.F.A) attached with Horses	
	9.5.19		Unit Chests 30 lbs issued to Inf. Battalions	
	10.5.19		1 Horse (Mange) sent to No 2 VES	
	11.5.19		1 OR (Sgt Williams) proceeds on leave to UK	
	12.5.19		13 Horses & 3 mules despatched by Train to ~~No~~ ~~2~~ 4 Sick Animals to No 2 VES	
	13.5.19		3 OR attached 2 for a Course of Dressing & Shoeing & one with Sick Horse	
	14.5.19		2 Animals x Despatched by Rail	
	15.5.19		1 OR attached with 2 Chargers	
	16.5.19		2 Animals & 1 man despatched to Rejoin own unit	
	17.5.19		2 Chargers & 1 man attached Horses for Training	
	18.5.19		Issued to 38 RFA 2 Horses & Sets of Appointments	
	19.5.19		2 Horses Class 2 to No 34 Vety Hospital by Rail	
	20.5.19		1 Horse issued to Capt [illegible] RAVC	
	21.5.19		2 Horses evacuated to No 2 VES	
	22.5.19		NIL	
	23.5.19		NIL	
	24.5.19		2 Horses & Appointments Returned from 38 RFA Bde	
	25.5.19		1 Horse (Charger) & 1 OR attached from 31 Warwick Bty for Training	
	26.5.19		2 Animals (Sick) sold to Butcher for food Amount 1372 MKS	
	27.5.19		Horses issued to [illegible] Fld Ambulance	
	28.5.19		Nil	
	29.5.19		Sgt Williams RAVC Returns from leave	
	30.5.19			
	31.5.19		2 Vety Sergeants attached to unit, despatched to field units for duty	

Hm

J [illegible] Capt RAVC
OC 18th MVS

A7092 Wt. W125 9/M1293 750,000 1/17. D. D & L. Ltd. Forms/C2118/14.

Confidential

War Diary

of

Capt Hill
OC 18 MVS

From 1-6-19
To 30-6-19

Vol: No XIII

18th
MOBILE VETERINARY
SECTION.
No. VA. 67.
Date. 2-7-19

Instructions regarding War Diaries and Intelligence Summaries are contained in F. S. Regs., Part II. and the Staff Manual respectively. Title pages will be prepared in manuscript.

WAR DIARY
or
~~INTELLIGENCE SUMMARY.~~
(Erase heading not required.)

Army Form C. 2118.

June 1919

Place	Date	Hour	Summary of Events and Information	Remarks and references to Appendices
Berg Gladbach	1.6.19		Vety Sgt attd 18 MVS & transferred to Rhn Unit	
	2.6.19		Surplus animals issued in the Div. Vety Stores Issued	
	3.6.19		1 OR & 2 Horses attached 4 Mules Issued to M.G. Coy	
	4.6.19		1 OR & 2 Horses detached	
	5.6.19		No 20095 Cpl Baker RAVC arrives from No 34 Vety Hospital as Reinforcement	
	6.6.19		Div. Races. Horse Ambulance in attendance	
	7.6.19		— Do —	
	8.6.19		nil	
	9.6.19		2 Horses & 2 Mules Issued in the Division	
	10.6.19		No TT/01507 Pte Hooker RAVC awarded 14 days "CB" 2 Sick animals sold to Butcher	
	11.6.19		No 14558 Sgt Derrett J. RAVC joins from No 34 Vety Hospital as Reinforcement	
	12.6.19		1 Mule Evacuated to No 2 VES	
	13.6.19		nil	
	14.6.19		nil	
	15.6.19		2 Animals attached for Treatment	
	16.6.19		No 28483 Pte VINE proceeds on leave to UK	
	17.6.19		1 Horse Sick collected with Horse Ambulance from 113 Bde RFA	
	18.6.19		1 Mule Sold to Butcher for Slaughter. 11 Sick Animals Evacuated by Train	
	19.6.19		6 Horses 5 Mules Evacuated to No 2 VES.	
	20.6.19		nil	
	21.6.19		Horses 3 Despatched to No 2 VES for disposal	
	22.6.19		1 Horse attached for a few days	
	23.6.19		Orders Recd to move in Evening Wagons packed & all ready by 6 PM. orders cancelled by 7.30	
	24.6.19		No 30681 Pte Tench proceeds on leave to UK	
	25.6.19		1 Sergt & 3 OR arrive from No 34 Vety Hospital for duties at Horse Dip	
	26.6.19		No 14558 Sgt Derrett despatched to No 39 MVS 1st Cav Div for duties	
	27.6.19		Rifle Drill & Training course for all Section men	
	28.6.19		nil	
	29.6.19		16453 SS Saward proceeds on leave to UK	
	30.6.19		Vety Sergt attached for duty. Float to 131 H Bty RGA for Sick Horse	J. Hill Capt RAVC OC 18th MVS

Confidential

War Diary

of Capt Hill

O.C. 18th MGS

From 1. 7. 19

To 31. 7. 19

Volume No XIII

Kimm

Army Form C. 2118.

WAR DIARY
or
~~INTELLIGENCE SUMMARY~~.
(Erase heading not required.)

Instructions regarding War Diaries and Intelligence Summaries are contained in F. S. Regs., Part II. and the Staff Manual respectively. Title pages will be prepared in manuscript.

July 1919

18th MOBILE VETERINARY SECTION. No. VR Date 2.8.19

Place	Date	Hour	Summary of Events and Information	Remarks and references to Appendices
Bere	1.7.19		No 15614 Sgt Alexander arrives as Reinforcement from No 1 MVS for Duty	
Glabbeek	2.7.19		nil	
	3.7.19		Pte Vine C Rave Returns from Leave	
	4.7.19		Dr Campbell RASC dispatched for Demobilization	
	5.7.19		1 Driver attached from Div Train. Rifle Firing course commences	
	6.7.19		nil	
	7.7.19		Inspection of Section & Full Kit	
	8.7.19		A DVS II Corps Visits Section	
	9.7.19		14 Sick Animals dispatched to No 2 VES.	
	10.7.19		nil	
	11.7.19		Pte Tench Rave Returns from Leave	
	12.7.19		Army Races Holiday for Half Men	
	13.7.19		No 20337 Pte Mitchell attached from No 24 Vety Hospital	
	14.7.19		1 Sick Horse sent to No 2 VES	
	15.7.19		1 Sick Horse collected by Horse Ambulance from Div Train	
	16.7.19		nil	
	17.7.19		S.S. Edwards returns from Leave	
	18.7.19		nil	
	19.7.19		Cpl Banks proceeds on leave to UK 20.7.19 to 3.8.19	
	20.7.19		Pte Smith proceeds on leave to UK 21.7.19 to 4.8.19	
	21.7.19		Sgt Watkins Rave attached from No 8 Vety Hospital	
	22.7.19		nil	
	23.7.19		1 attached man returned to Machine Gun Corps for Duties	
	24.7.19		Sgt Watkins Rave dispatched to 113 Bde for Duties as Vety Sergeant	
	25.7.19		nil	
	26.7.19		1 Horse classified E evacuated by Rail	
	27.7.19		nil	
	28.7.19		1 Horse dispatched to B/113 Bde RFA	
	29.7.19		NIL	
	30.7.19		NIL	
	31.7.19		NIL	

Div l of HQ RASC 20 18 MVS

A5992 Wt. W128.9/M1293 750,000. 1/17. D. D & I. Ltd. Forms/C2118/14.

Confidential

War Diary

of

Capt Eaga
OC 18th NDS

From 1. 8. 19
To 31. 8. 19

Vol No X VIII

Instructions regarding War Diaries and Intelligence Summaries are contained in F. S. Regs., Part II, and the Staff Manual respectively. Title pages will be prepared in manuscript.

WAR DIARY
or
~~INTELLIGENCE~~ SUMMARY.

(Erase heading not required.)

Army Form C. 2118.

August

Place	Date	Hour	Summary of Events and Information	Remarks and references to Appendices
~~[illegible]~~ Berg Gladbach	1.8.19		3 Horses to No 3 VES	
	2.8.19		Nil	
	3.8.19		1 Driver RASC despatched to No 1 Coy Train for Duties	
	4.8.19		Smith H RAVC Returns from leave	
	5.8.19		Pte Sammells proceeds on leave to UK	
	6.8.19		Nil	
	7.8.19		Pte Gray RAVC proceeds on leave to UK	
	8.8.19		1 RAVC Pte attached for duty from RFA	
	9.8.19		Nil	
	10.8.19		3 Mules despatched for Sale at Solingen	
	11.8.19		Cpl Bamber RAVC Returns from leave	
	12.8.19		4 Sick Animals to No 7 VES	
	13.8.19		Pte Chappell despatched to No 3[illegible] Vety Hospital for duties	
	14.8.19		Pte Thompson RAVC proceeds on leave to England	
	15.8.19		Nil	
	16.8.19		Nil	
	17.8.19		6 Horses despatched to No 2 VES	
	18.8.19		Nil	
	19.8.19		Nil	
	20.8.19		Pte Sammells RAVC Returns from leave	
	21.8.19		ADVS Visits Section	
	22.8.19		General Butler inspects the Section	
	23.8.19		Walker RAVC proceeds on leave to UK	
	24.8.19		Pte Gray RAVC Returns from leave	
	25.8.19		ADVS Visits Section. 2 Horses (WADVS) sent to Midland Div	
	26.8.19		Cpl Baker RAVC proceeds on leave to France	
	27.8.19		1 Horse and Mule sold to Butcher for Slaughter	
	28.8.19		Sgt Alexander Cpl Adams Cpl Bamber & Pte Manklow proceed for Demobilization	
	29.8.19		Pte Smith RAVC evacuated to 36 CCS from accident	
	30.8.19		Pte Willmott RAVC proceeds on leave to UK. Sgt Challand RAVC attached	
	31.8.19		Pte Thompson Returns from leave	

Edgar
Capt. RAVC
OC 18 M.V.S.

A7092 Wt. W 123/9 M1293 750,000. 1/17. D. D. & L. Ltd. Forms/C2118/14.

Confidential

War Diary

of

Major Bell

OC 18th MVS

From 1st 9. 19 To 30. 9. 19

Volume No. X 9.

Page 1

Instructions regarding War Diaries and Intelligence Summaries are contained in F. S. Regs., Part II. and the Staff Manual respectively. Title pages will be prepared in manuscript.

WAR DIARY
or
~~INTELLIGENCE SUMMARY.~~

(Erase heading not required.)

Sept 1919

Army Form C. 2118.

Place	Date	Hour	Summary of Events and Information	Remarks and references to Appendices
Bonn/ Gladbach	1-9-19		Capt Cagan takes over OC 18 MVS. 7 Animals to No 2 VES. S.S. Sawand proceeds for Dispersal. 1 Horse sold to Butcher	
	2-9-19		2 Horses sold to Butcher Sgt Richardson posted to 18 MVS	
	3-9-19		3 Sick Animals to No 2 VES	
	4-9-19		3 Sicks Animals to No 2 VES	
	5-9-19		5 Horses + 2 Mules dispatched to No 24 Vety Hospital for Sale	
	6-9-19		2 HD Horses sold to Butcher	
	7-9-19		S.S. Power RAVC posted to 18 MVS from No 24 V Hospital. Sgt Hemment proceeds for Dispersal	
	8-9-19		1 Mule sold to Butcher	
	9-9-19		Pte Walker RAVC proceeds on Leave to UK	
	10-9-19		2 Sick Animals to No 2 VES 2 Horses to No 24 Vety Hospital for Sale. 1 Horse Sold to Butcher	
	11-9-19		nil	
	12-9-19		1 Dr RASC posted to 18 MVS as 1st Line Transport Man	
	13-9-19		1 Horse Sold to Butcher	
	14-9-19		nil	
	15-9-19		1 Mule collected by Float & taken to Slaughter House for Destruction	
	16-9-19		nil	
	17-9-19		ADVS visits 18 MVS.	
	18-9-19		Pte Smith RAVC Returns from Hospital	
	19-9-19		Pte Walker RAVC proceeds on Leave to UK	

A7092 Wt. W128.9/M1293 750,000. 1/17. D. D & L. Ltd. Forms/C2118/14.

Instructions regarding War Diaries and Intelligence Summaries are contained in F. S. Regs., Part II. and the Staff Manual respectively. Title pages will be prepared in manuscript.

Page 2

WAR DIARY
or
INTELLIGENCE SUMMARY.
(Erase heading not required.)

Army Form C. 2118.

Sept 1919

Place	Date	Hour	Summary of Events and Information	Remarks and references to Appendices
Berg Gladbach		20.9.19	Nil	
		21.9.19	Nil	
		22.9.19	4 Sick Animals to No 2 V.E.S. 1 Mule Sold to Butcher	
		23.9.19	Privates: Hancocks, McNeill, Pain, Revell, & Sammells, proceed for Dispersal. Sgts. Stone Chisler & Watkins proceed for Dispersal	
		24.9.19	Cpl Strong RAVC proceeds on Leave	
		25.9.19	Major Bell takes over OC 18 M.V.S. Capt Edgar to Wermelskirchen	
		26.9.19	Sgt Challen RAVC proceeds for Dispersal	
		27.9.19	5 Horses dispatched to 'White City' Cologne for Dispersal	
		28.9.19	Nil	
		29.9.19	Hides of Horses destroyed Despatched to No 2 V.E.S.	
		30.9.19	6 Mules Received Sick. ADVS Visits Section	

W F Bell
Major RAVC
OC 18th M.V.S.

A7092 Wt. W128 9/M1293 750,000. 1/17. D. D & L. Ltd. Forms/C2118/14.

Page I

Instructions regarding War Diaries and Intelligence Summaries are contained in F. S. Regs., Part II. and the Staff Manual respectively. Title pages will be prepared in manuscript.

WAR DIARY
or
~~INTELLIGENCE SUMMARY.~~
(Erase heading not required.)

Army Form C. 2118.

18th MOBILE VETERINARY SECTION.
No. ......
Date 1. 11. 19.

Oct 1919.

Place	Date	Hour	Summary of Events and Information	Remarks and references to Appendices
Berg Gladbach	1.10.19		1 Horse & 24 Mules to No 24 V.E.S. for sale.	
	4.10.19		1 Horse from Div. H.Q. 1 Mule from No 2 D.A.C.	
	6.10.19		3 Horses & 3 Mules from 9th Glousters. 1 Horse to 9th Glousters.	
	7.10.19		3 Horses & 3 Mules to No 2 V.E.S.	
	8.10.19		Pte Scott M.G.C. Returned to C. Coy M.G.C.	
	9.10.19		4 Horses to No 2 V.E.S.	
	10.10.19		6 Animals to No 2 V.E.S.	
	12.10.19		Sgt Shalland RAVC. again proceeds for dispersal	
	13.10.19		12 Sick Animals to No 2 V.E.S.	
	14.10.19		4 Horses & 1 Foal from 2/1 Wk Bdy. 2 Horses from B/113 Bde.	
			1 Horse from Divn H.Q. Signal Coy. A.D.V.S. visits section.	
	15.10.19		9 Horses to No 2 V.E.S. (1 Horse from section 1 Foal)	
			Sgt Williams proceeds on 14 Days leave.	
	16.10.19		4 Horses 1 Mule from C/113 Bde. 2 Horses from A/H.A.C.	
			Pte Walker W. returns from leave. (A.D.V.S. visits section.)*	
	18.10.19		8 Animals to No 2 V.E.S. Dr. Johnson returns from leave.	

(A9475) Wt W2358/P360 600,000 12/17 D. D. & L. Sch. 52a. Forms/C2118/15.

* A.D.V.S. visits section 17.10.19.

Page 2

18th M.V.S.

Instructions regarding War Diaries and Intelligence Summaries are contained in F. S. Regs., Part II, and the Staff Manual respectively. Title pages will be prepared in manuscript.

Oct. 1919

WAR DIARY
or
~~INTELLIGENCE SUMMARY~~.
(Erase heading not required.)

18th MOBILE VETERINARY SECTION
No. ....
Date ....

Army Form C. 2118.

Place	Date	Hour	Summary of Events and Information	Remarks and references to Appendices
Berg Gladbach	18.10.19		1 Horse from B/113 Bde. 1 Horse from 84th Fld Amb.	
	19.10.19		1 Hide from 84th Fld Amb.	
	20.10.19		1 Hide sent to No 2 V.E.S. 1 Horse from H.Q. Sthn Div	
			S/S Power proceeds for dispersal. 1 Mule from 2/B. H.A.C.	
			S.S. Beachell joins 18 M.V.S vice Power.	
	21.10.19		1 H Horse from Sthn Divn Train.	
	22.10.19		Dr Fewlther R. R.F.A. proceeds for dispersal	
			Sgt Abbott RAVC proceeds for dispersal.	
			7 Mules recd from 1/5th Devons for inspection by Veterinary Officer (Retained)	
	23.10.19		Driver Johnson RFA sent on special leave.	
			Pte Walker A. proceeds for dispersal.	
	24.10.19		5 Animals to No 2 V.E.S. 2 Mules to Abbatoir Cologne.	
			A.D.V.S. visits section, also D.A.D.V.S. from Light Division.	
	25.10.19		1 Horse from 84th Fld Ambulance.	
			Cpl Bell, Pte Bewell, Pte Shimmons joins from No 21 M.V.S.	

(A9175) Wt W2358/P360 600,000 12/17 D. D. & L. Sch. 52a. Forms/C2118/15.

Instructions regarding War Diaries and Intelligence Summaries are contained in F. S. Regs., Part II, and the Staff Manual respectively. Title pages will be prepared in manuscript.

18th M.V.S. WAR DIARY
or
~~INTELLIGENCE SUMMARY~~.
(Erase heading not required.)

Oct 1919.

18th MOBILE VETERINARY SECTION.
No.........
Date.........

Army Form C. 2118.

Place	Date	Hour	Summary of Events and Information	Remarks and references to Appendices
Rur Gladbach	25/10/19		Driver Townsend R.A.S.C sent to Coy for demobilization	
	26/10/19		Pte Hammersley joins for duty from No 21 M.V.S.	
			Sgts Whitman and Reffell join for duty from Light Divn.	
	27.10.19		Sgt Martin joins for duty from Light Division.	
			Cpl Stroud re-joins from leave. A.D.V.S. visits section.	
			Sgt Riley & Cpl Pickers reports for duty from No 8 Vety Hospt.	
	28.10.19		Sgts Whitman, Reffell & Martin to No 8 Vety Hospital.	
			Cpl Bell sent to No 57 M.V.S. 12 Horses from No 1 Coy Train	
	29.10.19		Sgt Rox reports for duty and posted to 29th Bn M.G.C.	
			1 Horse from 2/113 Bde. 1 Horse from No 3 M.V.S.	
	30.10.19		Sgt Thurlow reports for duty with D.A.C.	
			6 Horses 1 Mule to No 8 Vety Hospt. 8 Horses to Tie Horses.	
			4 " from No 4 Coy Train. 14 Horses from No 3 Coy.	
			1 Pony from 1st Inf Bde. A.A.	
	31.10.19		17 Horses to No 8 Vety Hospt. 3 Horses from 51st Devons	
			1 " from 52nd Devons 1 Mule from 53rd Warwicks.	

W. Bell Lt R.A.V.C.
O.C. 18th M.V.S.

Instructions regarding War Diaries and Intelligence Summaries are contained in F. S. Regs., Part II. and the Staff Manual respectively. Title pages will be prepared in manuscript.

Page 4

Oct. 1919.

WAR DIARY
or
INTELLIGENCE SUMMARY
(Erase heading not required.)

18th MOBILE VETERINARY SECTION.
No.
Date

Army Form C. 2118.

Place	Date	Hour	Summary of Events and Information	Remarks and references to Appendices
Berg. Gladbach.				
	31. 10.19		Cpl Stroud proceeds for dispersal.	
	26.10.19		Pte Perkins granted 14 days leave. 27.10.19 to 10.11.19.	
	30.10.19		Ptes: Bennett, Barker, Cobb. Fenton, Burcott. Stevens, Swale, Fraquair posted from No 2 V.E.S to 18 M.V.S.	

(A9175) Wt W2358/P360 600,000 12/17 D. D. & L. Sch. 52a. Forms/C2118/15.

www.ingramcontent.com/pod-product-compliance
Lightning Source LLC
Chambersburg PA
CBHW081553160426
43191CB00011B/1919
* 9 7 8 1 4 7 4 5 1 4 6 9 9 *